Apple Watch Series 6 User Guide

The Latest 2020 Manual for Beginners, Kids, Teens, and Seniors On How To Master All The Special Features Of Apple Watch 6 & WatchOS 7 (3rd Edition)

Katrine Isaksen

Table of Contents

INTRODUCTION

Do you have an Apple Watch Series 6? If yes, how do you use it? What is the best way to get the most out of it?

Apple Watch Series 6 is a watch everyone must have, based on the capacity and the endowment of the watch.

Having the right amount of sleep is very key for good health. The new Sleep app helps you create a good regular bedtime routine and also keeps track of your daily sleep trends every night. It means that you can set and achieve your personal sleep goals daily.

Apple watch series 6 have an expansive Retina displays that has just been created by Apple, so as to enable you see more at a glance. Advanced sensors that keep you tracked all the ways you move. Robust powerful features that make you stay healthy and safe.

If it's your first time using Apple Watch, you may

experience some difficulty at first, because of its unique interfaces which is very different from iPhone and iPad. That is why this guide was put together to help you get used to the interface and find your way through the device.

This guide will show you the lineup, the step by step setup and operation of Apple watch series 6. You will also learn how to measure the oxygen level in your blood, how to Check your heart rate and set up your cycle tracking. It contains lots of Tips and Tricks in operating watchOS 7 and navigating the watch series 6.

CHAPTER 1

Apple Watch Series 6

The Apple Watch Series 6, was released in Sept 2020, which may be the current iteration of the Apple Watch that was initially launched in 2015. The Apple Watch Series 6 is similar in design to the Series 5, but there are a few notable health-related functions plus a quicker chip for much better performance.

There is a new sensor within the Apple Watch Series 6 that allows Blood Oxygen monitoring that steps O2 saturation within the bloodstream for better knowledge of fitness and wellness. When air saturation (also called SpO2) levels fall, it's rather an indication of a significant illness.

Blood oxygen supervising is enabled through 4 clusters of crimson, natural, and infrared LEDs alongside four photodiodes about the back from the Apple Series Watch, which gauge light reflected from the bloodstream. A custom made algorithm contained in the fresh Blood O2 app measures bloodstream O2 between 70 and 100. On-demand testing can be acquired with the app, as well as the watch also occasionally requires background measurements whenever an individual is inactive, which includes during sleep. Information comes in a medical app.

in the iPhone 11. It is 20% quicker, permitting apps to release 20% quicker, and it supplies the same all-day 18-hr battery life. Apple Watch Series 6 offers quicker charging and may be billed to complete in 1.5 hrs. Battery life continues to be improved for monitoring workouts like interior and outdoor operations, too.

Not used to the Apple Watch Series 6 may be the same U1 chip and Ultra-Wideband antennas introduced within the iPhone 11 choices, which Apple says allows short-range wifi location to aid new experiences such as digital Car Secrets. Apple offers the Series 6 with both Gps navigation and Gps navigation + LTE features. LTE Apple Watch versions can operate over LTE lacking any iPhone nearby.

This year's Apple Watch models can be found in aluminum, stainless, and titanium, with Apple introducing new blue and (Product)Red colorization choices for the aluminum models. Stainless Apple Watch versions come in metallic and a darkish gray graphite color, while titanium versions come in sterling silver and space dark.

Apple continuing to market Apple watch Nike and Apple Watch Hermès versions, with both featuring new music group options. Nike versions are available just in aluminum, while Hermès versions come in metal steel.

Alongside the Apple Watch Series 6, Apple introduced the lower-cost Apple Watch SE, which is priced starting at $279. The Apple Watch SE will be identical in style to the Apple Watch Series 6, nonetheless, it will be lacking several important features to help keep expenses down. It comes with an S5 chip that has been in the Series 5, nonetheless, it does not have an always-on screen, comes just in aluminum, does not have any blood air sensor, doesn't perform ECG readings, does not have any U1 chip, and doesn't assist 5GHz WiFi.

Besides that, it helps all fundamental Apple Watch efficiency such as heartrate monitoring, fall recognition, activity monitoring, crisis SOS, Apple Pay out support, sleep monitoring, water resistance, and much more. It will come in mobile and GPS choices similar to Series 6.

You can find three fresh Apple Watch band options this season, two of which eliminate closures and straps. The Single Loop and Braided Single Loop can be purchased in smooth silicon and braided yarn, respectively. Each one of these slips on the hands and onto the wrist, with Apple providing nine sizing choices. Gleam's new Leather Hyperlink band is a redesigned edition of the Natural leather Loop.

With the brand new Apple Watch designs and watchOS 7, Apple is introducing a family group Setup function that lets kids use Apple Watches without owning an iPhone. Mother and father can pair several Apple Watches with their iPhones for administration purposes, so kids may use the connection, safety, and health and fitness top features of the Apple Watch. There is a unique Activity ring encounter for children, and a fresh parental-controlled Usually Do Not Disturb mode known as School-time to greatly help kids stay concentrated and attentive while studying.

Apple Watch Series 6 and Apple Watch SE versions are for sale and to be purchase from the web Apple Store. Prices for the Series 6 begins at $399, while prices on the Apple Watch SE starts at $279. Apple is also carrying on to the market, the Apple Watch Series 3 prices starts at $199.

How to Buy

Apple Watch Series 6 can be bought from the web Apple

Shop and Apple shops as of Sept 18. Price for the Apple Watch Series 6 begins at $399 for non-LTE versions and $499 for LTE versions.

Prices vary predicated on instance material, strap, and collection, with entry-level prices for each material and dimension available below.

- 40mm Aluminium Non-LTE - $399
- 40mm Lightweight aluminum LTE - $499
- 44mm Lightweight aluminum Non-LTE - $429
- 44mm Metal LTE - $529
- 40mm STAINLESS (LTE only) - $699
- 44mm STAINLESS (LTE only) - $749
- 40mm Titanium (LTE just) - $799
- 44mm Titanium (LTE just) - $849
- 40mm Nike Non-LTE - $399
- 40mm Nike LTE - $499

- 44mm Nike Non-LTE - $429
- 44mm Nike LTE - $529
- 40mm Hermès (LTE just) - $1249
- 44mm Hermès (LTE just) - $1299

Apple Watch Series 6 models can be purchased in many nations all over the world, with prices that vary predicated on location.

Issues

Some Apple Watch owners using watchOS 7 have come across a problem that triggers missing GPS mapping information when recording workout, Other people have complained of significant electric battery life issues following an update. Like a repair, Apple indicates unpairing the Apple watch, resetting the iPhone completely, and restoring from the backup to handle the problem.

Reviews

Before the launch of the Apple Watch Series 6, members from the media could test it out there and shared their ideas with the audience. A lot of the evaluations of the brand new device have already been good, praising the brighter Always-On screen as well as the blood oxygen checking feature.

From testimonials, it's well worth noting that it could be difficult to obtain an accurate bloodstream oxygen reading as the band must be tight in the wrist as well as the arm must be held still.

Some reviewers were unsatisfied that the Series 6 didn't get them a notable upsurge in electric battery life, while some other reviewers were happy with the velocity of the brand new S6 chip.

Design

With regards to style, the Apple Watch Series 6 casing looks identical to the Apple Watch Series 5, featuring slim-bezel displays in 40 and 44mm dimension options to match several different wrists.

The Apple Watch Series 6 measures at 10.4mm solid and it is constantly on the feature, the same square-shaped design that Apple has used because of the Apple Watch released in 2015. Without design changes towards the situation, the Apple Watch Series 6 works together with all previous-generation Apple Watch bands.

Apple's 40mm versions measure 40mm large and 34mm wide, as the 44mm versions are 44mm great and 38mm wide. Weights range between 30.5 grams to 47.1 grams based on both dimension and casing materials, with the stainless Apple Watch choices becoming the heaviest.

All Apple watch Series 6 models include a dark ceramic and crystal that houses several sensors for heart rate monitoring, blood O2 supervising, and ECGs. Set alongside the Series 5, you can find twice as numerous

LEDs underneath. The Apple Series 6 provides four Directed clusters and four photodiodes to aid the health supervising features.

An Electronic Crown privately of the Apple Watch can be acquired for navigation reasons, and there is a Part Button that's used to bring up commonly used apps, access crisis services, confirm Apple Pay purchases, and much more.

The Digital Crown has haptic feedback that provides an accurate, mechanical feel when scrolling through lists and controlling various areas of the Apple Watch, which is key for that ECG app since it includes a built-in electrode that works in tandem using the sensors over the Apple Watch.

Remember that the Digital Crown appearance different with regards from the Apple Watch model you get. LTE models possess a reddish ring round the Digital Crown and that means you know that they will have LTE features, while GPS-only versions lack the reddish ring.

Always-On Display

Just like the Apple Watch Series 5, the Apple Watch Series 6 works for an OLED ultra-low strength temperature poly-silicon and oxide display (LTPO) make it possible for an Always-On Retina display, that allows time, complications, along with other information to be continually visible while using the screen no more leads to black interface once the Apple Watch isn't in use.

Using the Always-On display, you don't have to twist your wrist before you can see the time, so when utilizing the Workout app, workout metrics are visible all the time to keep an eye on metrics just to know how many calories you're burning, what lengths you've operate, and how long you've exercised.

The display dims once the wrist is down to be able to

preserve battery life, but key features like watch hands stay lit regularly. Touching the view face or raising the wrist brings the screen back to complete brightness, also to minimize battery drain, Apple offers optimized watch encounters for the function. The Apple Watch's display also offers an adjustable refresh price that falls from 60Hz to only 1Hz once the watch is inactive.

The Always-On screen from the Apple Watch Series 6 is 2.5 times brighter when outdoors once the wrist is down, rendering it simpler to see when working out in the bright sun. Additionally, there is an always-on barometric altimeter that continuously tracks elevation modifications in realtime for trekking, skiing, and comparable activities.

The Apple Watch Series 6 offers lots of the same screen specifications because of the Apple Watch Series 5, such as 1000 nits brightness. The lightweight aluminium Apple Watch models work on Ion-X glass to safeguard the screen, while stainless and titanium versions make use of sapphire crystal cup. Sapphire crystal cup offers a better scrape level of resistance than Ion-X cup because it is a harder material, this means the versions with sapphire crystal versions are proof of scratching and daily wear.

The 40mm Apple Watch Series 6 includes a resolution of 324 x 394 pixels, as the much larger 44mm Apple View Series includes a resolution of 368 x 448. This means a 759 mm^2 screen area for your 40mm Apple watch along with a 977 mm^2 screen area at the 44mm Apple watch.

Forget About Force Touch

Those people who have owned several versions of the Apple Watch are aware of the Force Touch gesture that popped up in interactive menus and settings when pressing down on the watch screen having a finger. Apple removed Force Contact in watchOS 7, therefore those gestures are usually no longer obtainable.

All the efficiency enabled by Force Touch is still accessible around the Apple View but through new swipe lower gestures. Generally, something that was previously possible with Force Touch can be carried out with a hand or the Digital Crown to scroll right down to access more configurations.

Clearing all notifications, for instance, can be carried out by swiping right down to the top from the notification listing. Composing a note in Messages is performed with the same swipe down actions.

watchOS 7 Gets rid of Force Touch Support From Your Apple Watch, Here's Everything That's Changed

In some instances, gestures are changed with new icons

you could tap, such as when accessing controls using the Camera app, or with new screens, it is possible to swipe between, as this may be the case when changing a Move Goal in the experience app. Additional options have already been moved to the app Settings, and regarding creating new watch faces, it has been swapped with an extended press gesture.

Casing Materials

The Apple Watch Series 6 will come in three components this season, with Apple eliminating the ceramic choice and giving aluminium, stainless, and titanium Apple Watch models. Aluminium Apple Watch versions are the least expensive, while titanium versions are almost all expensive.

Apple introduced two new lightweight aluminium colors this season: the royal blue tone along with an (Item) Crimson that's scarlet. The two brand-new colors are choices alongside the original silver, space grey, and gold colors.

Stainless Apple Watch choices can be purchased in metallic, precious metal, and graphite, which is a deep grey shade. The titanium versions can be purchased in a natural color (a grey-silver precious metal) and area black.

Aluminum Apple watch models are produced from completely recycled 7000 collection aluminium, are light-weight, inexpensive, and created for an active way of life, while stainless models are usually heavier, more costly, and created for everyday use rather than centred on activity.

Titanium Apple watch models provide durability from the stainless steel versions plus a brushed end, but are much lighter and resist staining. In comparison to stainless steel versions, titanium models possess darker, even more, matte colouring.

Both stainless and titanium choices feature sapphire crystal displays which are even more scratch resistant compared to the Ion-X cup useful for aluminium choices. Aluminium models can be found with and without LTE online connectivity, while stainless and titanium versions are LTE just without cheaper GPS just models available.

With regards to specific weights, the titanium models weigh 13% significantly less than the stainless models, which will be the heaviest from the Apple Watch models, and many from the Series 6 models certainly are a bit lighter compared to the Series 5 models. Weights of every model are usually below:

40mm

- Lightweight aluminium: 30.5 grams
- Stainless: 39.7 grams
- Titanium: 34.6 grams

44mm

- Lightweight aluminium: 36.5 grams
- Stainless: 47.1 grams
- Titanium: 41.3 grams

Water Resistance

Series 6 Apple Watch models are usually rated for immersion in water as deep as 50 meters because of seals and adhesives. The loudspeaker, which needs airflow to produce good sound, is a stage of ingress and has been made to expel water from itself making use of good vibrations after contact with moisture.

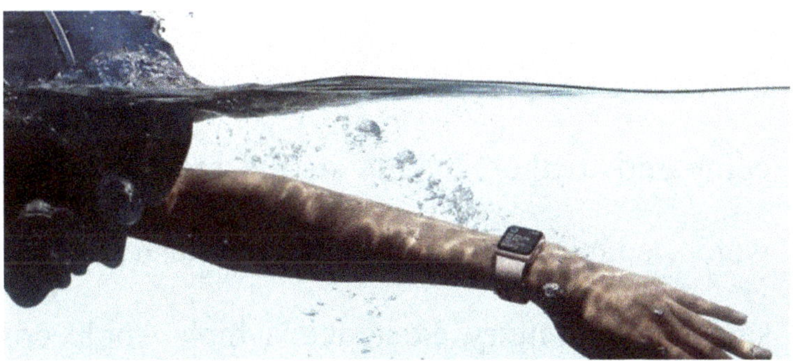

Since it is rated for 50m immersion, the Apple Watch

may be used when going swimming in the sea or in a pool. It is only suitable for shallow water actions, though, and can not be used for scuba, waterskiing, showering, or alternative activities that include high-velocity drinking water or heavy submersion.

Apple's Apple watch warranty will not cover water damage and mould, so it's best to be careful when exposing the watch to the water.

S6 Chip

There's a quicker dual-core S6 System in Package (SiP) in the Apple Watch Series 6, that is in line with the A13 Bionic processor found in the iPhone 11.

Following Apple, the S6 SiP is around 20% faster compared to the S5 chip in the prior-generation Apple watch, enabling apps to start 20% faster. It includes the same 18-hr battery existence, which Apple considers to be an "all-day" battery.

Health Features

Apple Watch Series 6 supplies the same wellness features obtainable in Series 5, plus bloodstream oxygen supervising. A second-generation optical heartrate sensor calculates metrics like calorie burn off, resting heart rate, and a heart rate that's high, and the electric heart rate sensor may be used when planning on taking electrocardiograms, while fresh LEDs and infrared lighting enable blood air monitoring.

An integral accelerometer and gyroscope enable additional important health-related functions such as drop detection.

The Apple Watch can detect a minimal heart rate, a higher heart rate, and an abnormal heart rate, monitoring for health issues like atrial fibrillation and delivering notifications when anomalies are detected.

Blood Air Monitoring

The sensors on the trunk of the Apple Watch enable the bloodstream oxygen supervising feature obtainable in the Apple Watch Series 6. Blood O2 saturation in an individual is just about 95 to completely, so when the portion of oxygen in the bloodstream falls below that, it could be indicative of a significant health issue that requires immediate attention.

Green, crimson, and infrared LEDs sparkle light onto the arteries in the wrist, with photodiodes measuring the quantity of light reflected again. Apple's algorithms after that calculate the color from the blood, which is a sign of just how much O2 is present.

Bright red bloodstream is very well oxygenated, whilst darker bloodstream has less air, which is how the Apple company Watch helps make its dedication about blood o2 level. Series 6 can gauge blood air between 70 and completely.

Blood oxygen dimensions could be taken in demand utilizing the brand-new Blood O2 app that's installed on the Apple watch. To have a measurement, make sure the Apple watch is snug within the wrist, open the app, stay still, and ensure that the wrist is smooth. Tap the start button and keep your arm still for 15 mere seconds.

By the end of the elapsed period, the Apple watch provides a reading through one's blood oxygen degree, with the info stored in the medical app for the iPhone.

The Apple Watch Series 6 also calls for some blood O2 measurements in the backdrop and this is established when the Apple Watch is established. These settings can be purchased in the medical app on iPhone. Tap Search > Respiratory > Bloodstream Oxygen > Setup Blood Oxygen.

Bloodstream oxygen dimensions happen if you find no motion, and predicated on your daily activity, the amount of readings each day and enough time between readings varies. Bloodstream oxygen measurements create a brilliant light over the wrist that may be distracting in black rooms, so history measurements could be switched off for Rest Mode and Theatre Mode if preferred with the Apple Watch's Configurations app.

During sleep, blood vessels oxygen measurements are just taken when the Monitor Rest with Apple watch option is allowed as well as when the watch has been used for Rest Tracking purposes.

The watch should be able to help to make a good connection with the top from the wrist by way of a snug wristband. Apple says that tattoo designs can impact overall performance, just as pores and skin perfusion, or the quantity of blood moving through your skin. In winter, for instance, readings could be affected.

Postures like getting the arm dangling at your part or fingers within a fist placement could cause unsuccessful dimensions, just as movement, and when the resting heart rate is over 150 beats every minute, the Apple Watch will not be able to give a successful blood air reading.

Following Apple, blood O2 measurements taken using the Apple watch Series 6 aren't designed for medical use and are created for "common physical fitness and wellness reasons." Because bloodstream oxygen monitoring will not require the same regulatory authorization as ECG readings, it is available in a lot more than 100 nations, with an inventory that may be on Apple's website.

ECGs

Electrodes in the rear of the Apple Watch, as well as the Digital Crown, interact to allow customers to consider single-lead electrocardiograms, like in Apple Watch Series 4. An ECG acts as an electrical exercise of the center and can be utilized to diagnose health issues by a physician.

ECGs are usually captured by keeping a finger on the

Digital Crown from the Apple Watch and will detect the sinus tempo (regular), a good abnormal result, or even, sometimes, a good inconclusive result that needs to be shared with a health care provider.

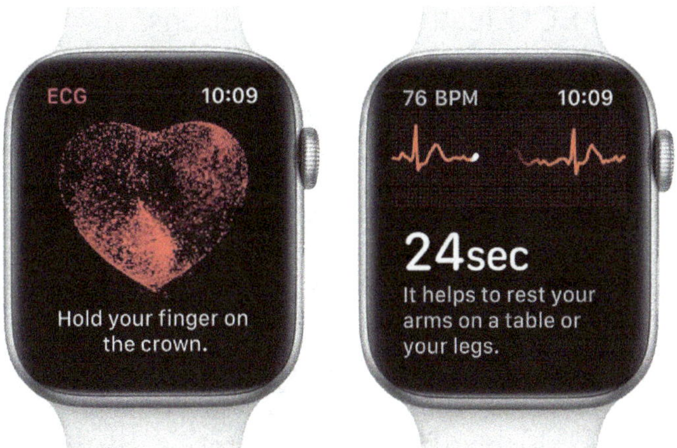

The single-lead ECG just like the Apple Watch means you can find two factors of getting in touch with measuring the electrical feelings of one's heart. Clinical electrocardiograms carried out by your physician might have 6 to 12 prospects for greater precision, but the Apple Watch supplies the convenience of having the ability to get an ECG anytime at any place in approximately 30 secs.

Because regulatory clearance is necessary for that ECG feature, it is limited to Apple Watch customers in selected nations, with an inventory on Apple's Feature Accessibility website. Apple is usually continually getting ECG features to new nations.

Sleep Tracking

With watchOS 7, the Apple Watch Series 6 could be worn during the night to keep track of your sleep, with Apple providing data on your long sleep every night. The function also offers useful tools so you can get an improved night's rest, with details obtainable in the Sleep Monitoring guide.

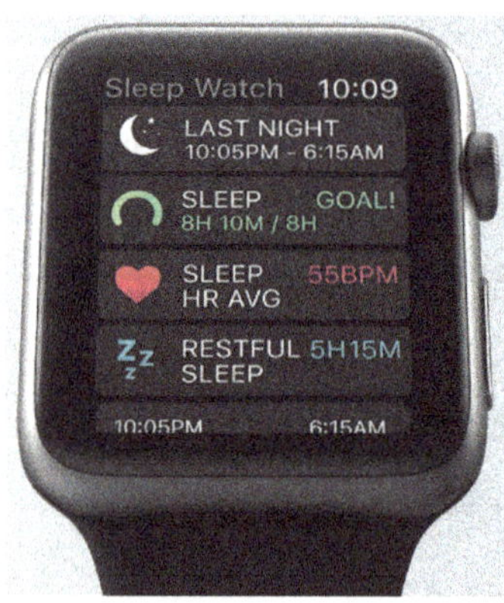

Sleep tracking can be acquired on older Apple Watch models as well, since it is enabled through software programs rather than equipment, but the Series 6 provides better battery effectiveness and faster charging to charge your Apple Watch quicker each day following a night's sleep.

Battery

Following Apple, the Apple watch Series 6 gives an all-day battery lifestyle of around 18 hours. The brand new Apple Watches charge quicker than ever, which is useful for functions like the sleep Tracking that has been launched in watchOS 7.

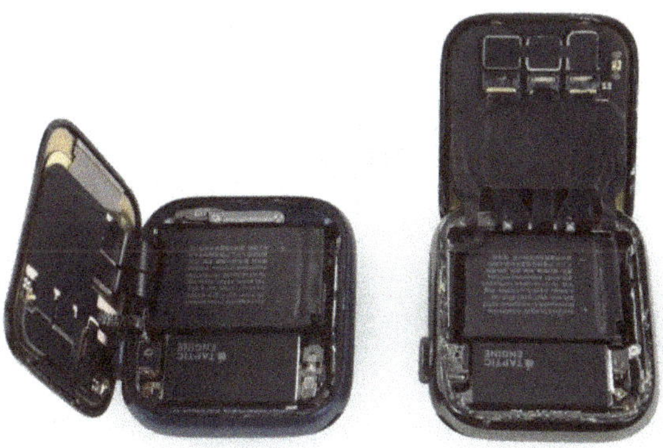

The 44mm Apple watch carries 1.17Wh electric battery that's 3.5% bigger than the battery in Series 5, as the 40mm Apple watch carries 1.024Wh electric battery that's 8.5% bigger than the battery in Series 5.

The brand new Apple Watch choices may charge to 80% in an hour or full in one and half hours. Using Series 5, a complete charge required 2.5 hrs. Battery life continues to be optimized for monitoring workouts like interior and outdoor operations.

Apple bases "all-day" electric battery life estimations on 90-period inspections, 90 notifications, 45 moments of the app use, along with a 60-moment workout with songs playback via Bluetooth. For LTE versions, Apple assumes four hours of LTE link and 14 hours of link with an iPhone.

In a few situations, the Apple Watch drains faster, such as

all the devices like a phone or when performing a workout. Listed below are Apple's electric battery life estimated for every activity:

- Sound playback from storage space - Around 11 hours
- Streaming audio more than LTE - Around 8 hours
- LTE talk period - Around 1.5 hours
- Family Setup battery Life - Around 14 hours
- Indoor exercise - Around 11 hours
- Outdoor exercise (GPS) - Around 7 hours
- Outdoor exercise (GPS + LTE) - Around 6 hours

Connectivity

Apple Watch Series 6 models include a good Apple-designed W3 chip, and you can find two variations available: Gps navigation and Gps navigation + Cellular. Gps navigation + Cellular versions have an integral LTE chip and may hook up to LTE lacking any iPhone, while Gps navigation models are Wi-fi only.

LTE

LTE connectivity continues to be available because the Apple Watch Series 3, sufficient reason for an LTE link, the Apple watch is untethered from your iPhone and will not require an iPhone or even known WiFi system for a web connection.

The Apple watch is not completely independent through the iPhone, though, because LTE connection through a provider requires an Apple watch and an iPhone 6s or later versions to talk about a cellular strategy with the same provider. The Apple watch doesn't have the battery capacity to be utilized full time on any iPhone nearby.

Apple watch LTE models can be purchased in many nations all over the world, with a complete listing on Apple's website.

U1 Chip

Apple added the U1 chip in the Apple Watch Series 6, which is the same Ultra Wideband chip that initially debuted in the iPhone 11 lineup. The U1 chip allows highly precise short-range cellular that Apple supports fresh experiences like Vehicle Keys, the function which allows an Apple watch (or iPhone) to be utilized instead of a physical vehicle key.

The U1 chip may be ideal for tracking Apple's upcoming AirTags which are likely to use U1 technology.

Emergency SOS

LTE connectivity allows an international Crisis SOS feature that has been first released using Series 5. With Crisis SOS, the Apple Watch could make worldwide calls to crisis services irrespective of where these devices were originally bought or if there's a dynamic cellular plan.

That means if you are traveling to a different country and

you are injured or in times where you will need help, it is possible to activate the SOS function in the Apple Watch by keeping the medial side switch to automatically speak to that country's crisis services.

International emergency calling works together with the Apple Watch's fall detection feature, so if's enabled, it automatically places a crisis call when the watch senses an individual has taken a difficult fall and remains motionless afterwards.

Wireless, Bluetooth, and GPS

Apple Watch Series 5 works with 5GHz 802.11b/g/n Wi-Fi (starting from 2.4GHz in the Series 5) and Bluetooth 5.0. In comparison to Bluetooth 4.2, Bluetooth 5.0 presents longer variety, faster speeds, bigger broadcast message capability, and much better interoperability with other wi-fi technologies.

Gps navigation has been contained in the Apple Watch because the Series 2, and all Series 6 versions, LTE and non-LTE, include a Gps navigation chip which allows the Apple Watch to find its place without having to be near a good iPhone.

With GPS, the Apple Watch can track rate, distance, and path you are walking, operating, hiking, or biking, providing more insight into your health and fitness activities. Gps navigation, GLONASS, Galileo, and QZSS techniques are backed for positioning technologies across multiple nations.

Other Features

Sensors

Apple Watch Series 6 functions electrical and optical heartrate receptors, LEDs and infrared lighting for blood air monitoring, the next-generation accelerometer useful for drop detection among other activities, a gyroscope, a good ambient lighting sensor, and a far more battery-efficient barometric altimeter to monitor flights of stairways climbed, elevation benefits when climbing, and much more.

Compass

There is a built-in compass along with a Compass app that allows customers to see they are going, incline, latitude, longitude, and current elevation. Compass features are included in the Maps app to allow users to observe which method they're dealing with when getting instructions.

Storage Space

Apple Watch Series 6 models have 32GB of space for storage for songs and apps.

No Energy Adapter

The 2020 Apple Watch models usually do not feature a 5W power adapter in the box-like prior Apple Watch choices, with Apple counting on visitors to use their existing power adapter options. Apple does continue steadily to provide an Apple Watch getting puck and wire alongside the Apple Watch.

Nike and Hermes Models

The Nike Apple Watch was made with Nike and was designed for runners. Nike Apple Watch models are made from metal and they cost the same just as the regular aluminium Apple Watches.

Nike has designed specific software for your Nike Apple Watch, that is made to motivate runners to remain active.

Nike Apple Watches include unique Nike-designed watch faces and are obtainable in silver and black aluminium with matching perforated bands or Sport Loops in an array of different Nike-exclusive colors.

The Hermès Apple Watch Series was made with French fashion house Hermès and features a few of the most expensive Apple Watches Apple offers due to the high price of the bands.

All Hermès choices feature a metallic or room black stainless Apple Watch body paired with the Hermès signature hand-crafted leather bands and yet another orange Hermès-branded Apple Watch Sport band. Hermès Apple Watches include unique watch faces predicated on Hermès watch designs.

Available

Apple offers designed in various types of bands of the Apple Watch, which it up-dates frequently, debuting new music group options **Bands** during drop and spring press events.

Apple offers an Apple Watch Studio function which allows most rings to be paired with most Apple Watch casing choices, so specific Apple Watch music group and casing pairings are usually no more required when coming up with a purchase.

Available bands are the Sport Band, Sport Loop, Milanese Loop, Contemporary Buckle, Link Bracelet, Leather Link, and brand-new Single Loop and Braided Single Loop that arrived alongside the Series 6.

Solo Loop

The Activity Loop is comparable to the Sports Music group, but it is the first Apple Watch to include a slip-on design without buckle or clasping mechanism. It's created from a stretchy liquid silicon rubber that may stretch to match over the hands and collapse to match tightly for the wrist.

Apple says that it is ultra-comfortable because you can find no overlapping components, and it's easy to wear and off. It's swim-proof, sweat-proof, and handled with UV for any silky complete. The Single Loop will set you back $49, and unlike all the other Apple watch band styles, it will come in nine various sizes for every watch casing dimension.

Apple supplies a printable dimension guide to find the design that best suits your wrist, moreso you should use the measuring tape to check on wrist dimension. You need to be sure to get a good dimension before ordering due to several dimension options.

Some people experienced fit problems with the Single Loop as well as the Braided Single Loop gave the precise sizing requirements, which includes prompted Apple to supply more tailored in shape instructions. Apple furthermore warns that this Single Loop can stretch out a bit as time passes due to the material that it's made of. Apple does allow earnings of the music group if you want a different dimension, but you need to get yourself a good suit in the first place.

Braided Single Loop

Just like the Solo Loop, the Braided Solo Loop is a new Apple watch designed without a buckle or clasp of any sort. It's designed from a stretchable recycled yarn interwoven with silicon threads so that it can match over the hands before wrapping around the wrist.

Apple states the soft, textured sense of the music group is perspiration and water-resistant, also ultra-comfortable to use. The Braided Single Loop can be purchased in nine dimensions for each Apple Watch casing dimension, so wrist dimensions are one of the things to look out for when you order (or you can find fitting choices in Apple's shops).

The Braided Single Loop is among Apple's most costly band options at $99, and the same sizing caveats connect with the Braided Single Loop.

Sport Band

Apple's Sports Rings will be the company's lightest, preferred bands, created from the flexible and light-weight fluoroelastomer. Because they're perfect for use when working out or participating in strenuous activity, the majority of Apple's aluminum timepieces ship with Sports activity Bands.

Pricing starts from $49 for the activity Bands, that can come with 3 pieces to regulate the size. Apple offers Sports Rings in S/M, M/L, and L/XL dimension options.

Sport Loop

Designed to be soft, breathable, and lightweight, the activity Loop is manufactured out of fabric that wraps around the wrist for a good but comfortable suit.

It's created from the velcro-like double-layer nylon and will come in a variety of colors, with Nike-branded Sports activity Loops also available. The 40mm edition fits wrists size ranges frome 130mm to 190mm, as the 44mm edition fits wrists size ranges from 145mm to 220mm. Apple costs $49 for the activity Loop.

Nike Band

The initial perforated Nike Apple Watch bands that include Nike watches may also be available on a standalone basis.

Nike bands are produced from the high-performance fluoroelastomer and so are designed for both 40mm and 44mm Apple Watch models, as well as Apple sells Nike-branded sports activity Loop options in unique shades. The bands in shape wrists size ranges from 130mm to 200mm. Nike Rings will set you back $49.

Milanese Loop

The stainless Milanese Loop, obtainable in 40mm and 44mm sizes, is a flexible metal mesh music group that wraps around the wrist. It's manufactured from such a good metal material that it is comfortable to put on for a whole day, and it's remarkably lightweight.

The Milanese Loop will cost you $99, morealso it come in silver, gold, and space black.

Leather Loop

The Buckskin Loop, designed from quilted Venezia natural leather, is another band that wraps around the wrist rather than using a clasp. They have two items, with one serving by way of a loop in another and magnetically attaching to itself to get a secure match. It's coming in at $99 and is designed for 44mm pieces. The Natural leather Loop matches wrists size ranges from 150mm to 210mm.

Leather Link

The Leather Hyperlink is new alongside the Apple Watch Series 6. It's like the Set Loop, but with a two-piece style that doesn't include a loop. The Buckskin Link is manufactured out of Roux Granada buckskin sourced from France and contains flexible, shaped magnets that cover around the wrist for a comfortable fit.

While the Set Loop isn't readily available for small 40mm Apple Watch, the redesigned Set Link fits both 40mm and 44mm models. It will come in small/moderate and moderate/large and suits wrists size from 130mm to 180mm.

Modern Buckle

The Present Day Buckle, created from supple Granada natural leather, is a music group that's made to use small 40mm Apple watch models. It includes a two-piece magnetic buckle and an internal coating of Vectran weave for power and scratch opposition.

Link Bracelet

The 316L stainless alloy Link Bracelet, obtainable in 40mm and 44mm sizes, is Apple's priciest band made in-house. Obtainable in sterling silver ($349) and area black ($449), the hyperlink Bracelet resembles a high-quality conventional watch band.

The 40mm magic size fits wrists sized 135mm to 195mm as the 44mm super model tiffany Livingston fits wrists sized 140mm to 205mm. A 6-hyperlink add-on package expands its dimension from 205mm to 245mm for yet another $49.

Hermès

Alongside Hermès Apple Pieces, Apple sells an array of standalone Hermès rings, designed by the style house. Hermès rings can be purchased in a variety of colors.

As they are rings created together with French-style houses, prices tend to be more expensive than Apple's rings. Hermès rings begin at $340 and rise from there.

Apple watch SE and Series 3

Alongside the Apple Watch Series 6, Apple introduced the Apple Watch SE, which is a new low-cost choice that offers lots of the same features as the Series 6, but with a far more affordable price. It is, nevertheless, lacking some crucial health functions to keep prices low.

Set alongside the Series 6, the Apple watch SE does not have ECG and blood vessels oxygen monitoring help which is furnished with a mature S5 chip rather than the faster S6 chip. It is only obtainable in aluminium, the least expensive and lightest from the Apple watch casing materials.

Besides that, they have the same safety and health monitoring functionality, which is obtainable in LTE and GPS models. Prices in Apple Watch SE starts at $279 to $399 for that Series 6.

Being an ultra-low-cost choice, Apple continuing to market the Apple watch Series 3, priced start at $199. The Series 3 comes with an old design with an inferior display, a very much slower S3 chip, no bloodstream O2 sensor or ECG functionality. It is Gps navigation only and does not have additional great features like an always-on altimeter and compass which are present in the other Apple Watch models.

Apple Watch Series 6 vs. Apple Series Watch SE Buyer's Guide

Apple Watch Series 5 vs. Series 6 Buyer's Guide

Apple Watch SE vs. Apple Watch Series 3 Buyer's Guide

watchOS 7

Apple Watch Series 6 and Apple Watch SE versions run an operating-system called watchOS and include watchOS 7 installed.

The watchOS 7 update includes several new watch faces, like a GMT watch face that presents multiple time areas, Total for tracking elapsed time, Chronograph Pro using a tachymeter, Typograph for displaying numerals in custom styles, Artist with art by Jeff McFetridge, Memoji for putting a Memoji on Apple Watch, and Stripes in customizable patterns.

A Sleep app enables you to track your sleep by wearing your watch during the night, providing rest analysis in a straightforward, easy-to-interpret format. The watch uses the accelerometer to identify subtle movements connected with breathing so that it knows if you are sleeping or awake.

A Wind-Down function helps you set up a healthy bedtime program, while Sleep Setting automatically converts your display and enables ***Usually Do Not Disturb***. Once you are awake, the Apple watch plays soft noises or runs on the haptic alarm, also it gives up a climate report and battery information to start your day.

watchOS 7 provides a Family Set up option that let the iPhone proprietors manage and setup Apple Timepieces for children or even older family who don't own iPhones. Moms and dads control connections and downloaded apps, there is a Schooltime setting to limit Apple Watch functions when required, and location monitoring with Discover My location can be acquired.

With Family Setup, kids can call and text their mother and father, speak to Siri, stream songs, download apps, use the new Memoji app to generate Memoji, and use Apple Pay out with funds supplied by moms and dads. Family Sharing also contains Activity tracking options that provide Proceed minutes rather than active calories burnt, and activity monitoring continues to be optimized for kids.

There is a handwashing recognition feature that's useful

because we are all washing our fingers more regularly than usual. It enables the Apple watch to listen for noises of water and starts a 20-2nd timer to remind you to clean the hands for the correct timeframe.

The Experience App continues to be renamed Health and fitness and there is a refined interface, and afterward this season, the Physical fitness app works with the new Health and fitness+ support that permits Apple Watch owners to access guided workouts on Apple TV, iPhone, and iPad. The brand new Physical fitness app also enables customers to customize Exercise goals, including Having hours and Workout minutes, as well as the Apple Watch, can gauge low-range VO2 maximum, stair ascent acceleration, stair descent swiftness, and six-minute stroll estimate, which are available in the medical app.

Apple also introduced a fresh Siri Shortcuts app for your Apple Watch to access all of your Shortcuts directly on your wrist.

watchOS 7 will help to safeguard hearing health by having a regular hearing notification and a choice to automatically reduce loud noises when you're putting on headphones. The greatest extent volume setting helps to avoid hearing damage.

Future Apple watch Rumours

Rumours indicate another version from the Apple Watch may adopt solid condition control keys that don't physically click on but rather provide haptic comments to users once the control keys are usually touched, but it isn't clear when that is approaching. Apple introduced haptic suggestions at the Digital Crown in the Series 4, and haptic opinions could potentially be lengthened aside button in a later Apple Watch model.

Further, in the foreseeable future, the Apple Watch can do without buttons completely, with the edges of these devices adopting help for contact and swipe-based gestures.

Apple is rumoured to truly have a group of biomedical technicians working on a way for non-invasively supervising blood glucose amounts using optical detectors, a technology which could potentially help make its way into the Apple Watch sooner or later in the foreseeable future. Such a function would make diabetes management easier because it wouldn't require puncturing your skin.

Apple reportedly includes a secret manufacturing unit in a Santa Clara, Ca where it is developing and producing check samples of shows that make use of microLED, a technology that may follow OLED. microLED displays can lead to devices that are thinner, brighter, and make use of less power. Gossips suggest an Apple Watch having a microLED screen could be release in 3 or 4 years.

Patents

Apple offers patented several interesting systems that could potentially be used in future Apple Watch devices, like a biometric authentication function that authenticates identification in line with the wearer's epidermis pattern. This type of function would get rid of the dependence on passcode when putting on the Apple watch.

Another patent describes the self-tightening Apple Watchband that could adjust during intensive pursuits like jogging or training for accurate heart rate readings, and take it easy afterward. The tensing may be used for instructions, workout reps, and much more.

Another patent describes an Apple Watchband having an LED indicator that could visualize the improvement of a task or job, providing a visible indicator when concluding a good work out or a task ring, for instance.

Apple in Dec 2019 published the patent describing the way the Apple Watch may help physicians monitor the outward symptoms of Parkinson's on individuals using sensors to help keep tabs on tremors. Apple believes this technique of data monitoring will allow customers to better monitor their symptoms to allow them to plan routines around symptom designs.

Apple has filed other patents for moving hardware into the Apple Watch's music group, including batteries, loudspeakers, kinetic energy generators, haptic responses devices, and also cameras.

There is no word on whether these trademarked features can make it into a genuine Apple Watch, but it's interesting to find out what Apple will be focusing on and considering behind the moments.

CHAPTER 2

Situation and Connection - Force Touch

The brand new eye-catching functions are new colors, in particular, the brand new glowing blue and red aluminium case, and the brand new solo loop rings.

As before the lightweight aluminium models function Ion-X glass as the stainless and titanium versions include Sapphire cup instead. The LPTO OLED that has been firstly introduced using the Watch Series 4 continues to be well functional in sunlight. Following Apple, its Always-On Display's optimum brightness continues to be enhanced by 2.5x on the watch Series 5, which is said to be beneficial mostly to those that cannot increase their arm throughout their workout for reasons unknown. We were amazed by how quick the new gadget switched between your two modes. Despite having Always-On Display allowed activating the whole display when raising your arm requires a split second.

The trunk side continues to be updated to add the brand new sensor. The brand new sensor variety is made up of a crystal with four picture diodes and four natural/reddish/infrared Directed clusters. This variety now permits estimating your bloodstream oxygen level in addition to measuring and documenting your heart rate, your heart tempo, and identify when you're asleep. The second option does not need the brand new sensor and it is thus on all versions that may be up-to-date to watchOS 7, specifically Series 3 and newer version.

Nevertheless, updating to watchOS on previous Apple watch models comes at a cost. The most recent iteration of Apple's cellular operating system no longer supports Force Touch, which in earlier versions was utilized to access framework selections or customize the presently installed watch encounters. Instead, this manner of input has been now partly changed with an extended touch without using extra pressure. The Apple watch Series 6 does not have the Force Touch gasket that has been existing on previous versions, on all old products, its readings are simply just ignored.

The Apple Watch Series 6 helps GPS and it is ISO 22810:2010 licensed against ingress of water around 50m. The brand new Wi-Fi chip right now also facilitates 5 GHz rings. Furthermore, the watch includes NFC for Apple Pay and a loudspeaker and mic for Siri and calls. As before, an LTE design with eSIM assistance can be acquired optionally at reduced.

Set up and Handling

Setting up an Apple Watch cannot be finished with an Android smartphone since it takes a compatible iPhone.

Nevertheless, because of watchOS 7's fresh family setup function, this doesn't need to be your personal iPhone. The Watch app is necessary for pairing and setting up the Apple watch will be preloaded on any iPhone automatically and have the capacity of controlling multiple watches if required.

The Watch itself includes numerous preloaded applications, such as a remote-control application for the iPhone's camera. Among the Apple, Watch's largest advantages will be its App Shop ecosystem with a big selection of third-party programs. If an iPhone app furthermore happens to aid the Apple Watch, it is instantly set up on a suitable Watch as well, so long as this feature continues to be enabled.

The watch faces could be customized either via the watch app on the iPhone or in the watch itself. Altering between the numerous installed watch encounters may be accomplished with horizontal swipes over the display. The electronic crown can be used for scrolling through configuration selections or zooming in the Pictures app. The solitary button may be used to either screen the Dock, which consists of all recently utilized applications, or perhaps a customizable set of favorite apps.

All this isn't new at all. Its simplicity is among the basic principles determining the Apple Watch, as may be the complete integration of several Apple products logged along with the same Apple ID collectively. For instance, should Siri react to your questions having a research and website recommendation you can open up this website on your Mac PC because of Handoff. Also, all Siri recommendations and open web sites are synchronized with your Macintosh found in Safari's background. Also, you can even use your Apple Watch to unlock your Mac

PC. Once set up the watch will vibrate and have fun with an audio reminiscent compared to that of the vault opening each time it unlocks your Macintosh. A nice contact for sure.

Notifications and Telephony

Automagically, the Apple watch mirrors your iPhone's notification configurations, which may later be on customized and modified to your liking. WhatsApp communications will screen emojis but just a blurry preview of pictures. Replies can contain either predefined blocks of textual content, emojis, a dictated information, or perhaps digitized information with each notice scribbled onto the watch's screen. New messages can only be delivered as text, much less WhatsApp meaning. This is true for all other messengers that don't provide a native Apple watch app.

You can have a phone call directly from the watch on

your wrist, and you may also make calls through either your contacts, your recent call history, or perhaps a dial-pad. As the LTE design is with the capacity of working independently from the iPhone it is paired towards the Gps navigation/Wi-Fi design requires the iPhone to stay close-by.

Health - Finally with SpO2 Sensor

Fitness buffs like the Apple watch and the medical sector has been impressed by the Apple Watch Series 4's ECG function. And while additional OEMs appear to struggle with dependable ECG information - Samsung's execution, for example, had been delayed frequently and continues to be unavailable in lots of countries, which includes Germany, even today - a growing amount of wearables start featuring blood O2 saturation (SpO2) detectors capable of discovering possible anti snoring. Apple, alternatively, only backed heart rate and rate of recurrence (ECG) metrics in addition to an app for listening to wellness. With watchOS 7, a rest tracker is currently finally designed for all backed Apple Pieces (Series 3 and Series that follows), as well as the Apple Watch Series 6 finally works with blood air saturation monitoring.

Heart Frequency, Heart Rate, and O2 Saturation

Automatically, the ECG app isn't on an Apple watch. Instead, it should be correctly setup in the iPhone's Wellness app where you can decide whether you need constant and automated or manual heart rate and blood O2 readings. If the watch detects atrial fibrillation, which is often associated with an increased threat of struggling a stroke, it'll issue a caution.

Heart frequency dimensions have become accurate. In our research, Apple watch was with the capacity of precisely measuring coronary heart regularity both when idle and training with increasing overall performance, and it's documented values almost similar to that of the heart rate of the upper body strap. When examining the workout information, we found nearly identical data conserve for an individual heartbeat.

Normally, blood oxygen levels data differed from that documented by a licensed pulse oximeter by simply 1.5% with no more than around 3%. Utilizing the Bloodstream Oxygen app on your watch you can start a manual reading through your bloodstream oxygen. If required the watch can automatically get readings many times a day even though you are asleep. The matched iPhone's Wellness app will graph that information during days, several weeks, or months.

Sleep Tracking

For the very first time in the annals of watchOS, the brand new version 7 natively supports sleep tracking during the night. However, in comparison with sleep tracking information recorded by gadgets like the Samsung Galaxy watch 3, the Fitbit Feeling, or Huawei wearables like the Recognition Magic watch 2 or TicWatch Pro 3 Gps navigate that Apple's data will be poor at greatest. The tracker will not be capable of correctly distinguishing your sleep phases (gentle sleep, deep rest, REM rest) in one another.

What it is capable of saving is the time you fell asleep, time you woke up, and how often you are awoke during the night. This information could be graphed and analyzed long-term during the last couple of days and will let you know if you arrived at your self-defined sleep objective for weekdays and weekends. Even though heart rate and air saturation information is available for the same time frame a sleep diagram overlay isn't available. Furthermore, unlike Fitbit's algorithms, Apple's infrequent readings will undoubtedly be barely in a position to reliably detect anti snoring.

It was suspected that more regular readings would reduce the Apple Watch's battery life further. Cost levels below 30% can lead to caution. How and why the Apple Watch Series 6 were able to record additional time rest than time spent during intercourse continues to be a secret to us.

Activity Rings

Another Apple watch feature is its capability to motivate customers to invest less time sitting and much more time moving using its Exercise app. Standing up is primarily targeted at staying away from long-term seated and requires you to get up at least one time each hour and manoeuvre around for a minimum of one minute.

The exercise goal can best be reached through workouts that may be recorded using the preinstalled Workout app. If you're not a big lover of gyms or interior sports facilities, it is possible to alternatively achieve your everyday exercise objective and near the ring using a 30-moment long brisk stroll. Whatever you can report with the Exercise app or any Apple Health-compatible health and fitness app will count number towards your workout objective. The app may also calculate your daily calories with the addition of all workouts, steps used, etc. The app shop contains several apps that enable you to report your calorie consumption as well and make use of that data given into the Wellness app to report and monitor your body weight.

Workout Tracking

During writing, Apple's Workout app supported somewhat significantly less than 100 different exercises. Running could be paused immediately if you cease or by hand by pushing the electronic crown and part button simultaneously and terminating the exercise via touch switch on the screen.

Thanks to the built-in Gps navigation the watch is with the capacity of saving your track still lacking any iPhone present. Songs and audiobooks which have been formerly synchronized with your watch to be performed during your exercise on any suitable Bluetooth headset.

Today's workouts are available in the app for the watch. Analyzing older workout routines requires the Fitness and well-being app in the combined iPhone. The last-mentioned will even screen heart rate and frequency throughout your exercise session in addition to the relaxing period immediately later on. Unfortunately, this information is also available for the previous day.

Various choices to Apple's Workout app can be purchased in the app store, such as Strava or various other apps targeted at operating, going swimming, or golfing. Those apps are excellent for maintaining long-term records to be able to make use of these metrics for enhancement.

Verdict - The Brand New Hardware is fantastic, the Software Encounter Is Not

Making and receiving phone calls, listening to songs, downloading popular apps from your app store - the Apple Watch has benefits indeed. Nevertheless, is changing to the brand new Series 6 justifiable if you currently own a mature model?

The SpO2 sensor's information is more reliable on a great many other products. Furthermore, the Apple watch allows you to have both guide and automated readings enabled, that is seldom found on its rivals. Among others, one particular contender may be the Garmin Forerunner 745. The optical centre frequency sensor ended up being exact and accurate as well. The Apple Watch's SpO2 sensor is a high-quality sensor. After that, the variations to the Apple Watch Series 5 are small at best.

Switching through the AW5 is only going to pay off if you're interested in the excess health data supplied by the SpO2 sensor. In addition to the Apple Watch Series 6 Apple also list two versions without SpO2 sensor, ECG sensor and always-on screen: The Apple Watch Series 3, Starting from $199, and the Apple Watch SE, starting from $279.

The Apple watch Series 6 with 44mm screen currently starts at $429 plus tax with various merchants offering lower prices and holiday sales. Aside from Samsung's Galaxy Watch 3, which costs between $400 and $500 as well, almost every other wearables are much cheaper.

CHAPTER 3

Apple Watch Series 6 vs. Fitbit

The Apple Watch Series 6 and Fitbit are top smartwatches that will help monitor your fitness ranges and become a cell phone alternative on your wrist. Both likewise have an electrocardiogram (ECG or EKG -- Apple makes use of ECG) app, monitor workouts, rest and blood air amounts, but they're various in the manner each goes about doing these exact things. To help you to decide on what is right for you, I've compare them from physical fitness tracking to battery life and efficiency.

When you have an Android cell phone, the Fitbit can be your only choice, but both use iOS devices, choosing trickier when you have an iPhone. If you'd like the best general smartwatch, with smooth fitness monitoring and safety functions, get the $399 (£379, AU$599) Apple Watch. If you'd like the most strong sleep tracking, heat sensor and the very best battery life, get the $329 (£299, AU$499) Fitbit Feeling.

Apple Watch Series 6

The latest Apple Watch includes a robust group of fitness tracking features, an FDA-cleared ECG, blood oxygen tracking and all of the responsiveness you may need from the smartwatch. It is the better choice if you want built-in LTE to utilize your watch without your iPhone close by.

Fitbit

A good fitness watch for sleep tracking and battery performance

The Fitbit Feeling offers an FDA-cleared ECG, strong sleep tracking, a temperature sensor along with stress tracking sensor. Unlike the Apple Watch, also, it works with Google android, has a lot of third-party watch faces to select from, and offers the higher battery lifetime of both watches.

Both are comfortable to wear, with common designs.

The Series 6 appears like almost every other Apple Watch which has come before it, having a square face obtainable in two sizes (either 40mm or 44mm) and also an electronic crown and side button. The Feeling appears like a higher-end Versa and will come in just one single 40mm size having a stainless rim around the rectangular face, but rather of the physical key, it comes with an indentation privately that vibrates when pressed and may be used to regulate the display. As the Fitbit will be physically bigger than the 40mm Apple Watch, the specific display screen size is a hair larger than the Apple Watch due to the bezels. The Apple Watch also offers bezels around the display, although they're thinner than those around the Sense.

Each watch includes a colour, always-on display screen that's easy to understand in large daylight, although it was discovered that the Apple watch takes the advantage for general brightness when glancing straight down within my wrist during a patio exercise.

The Feeling has a lot more watch faces to select from than the Apple Watch, including third-party ones. Nevertheless, you can also customize some Apple Watch faces to add complications, which act like shortcuts: They can display information such as climate or calendar instantly. Both have various colours and equipment finishes to select from.

Straps on both are usually an easy task to swap in and out with a quick-launch buttons and you may change the appearance with a multitude of bands including natural leather, woven and silicon options.

Fitbit has added detectors, but you might not need them

Each watch may scan for possible indicators of a coronary heart situation called atrial fibrillation or aFib making use of their ECG apps. Spot your finger within the electronic crown for 30 secs on the Apple Watch, when you locate your catalogue and thumb on the contrary corners from the Fitbit for the same timeframe to have a reading.

You can talk about outcomes from both with your physician. Observe where the ECG can be acquired all over the world on the Apple watch and the Fitbit Feeling. Each watch may also keep track of for indications of higher or low heartrate and inform you accordingly.

Both may also monitor SpO2, or bloodstream oxygen saturation when you sleep. Check ranges in the medical app on your iPhone for that Apple watch, or await the Fitbit to determine your nightly typical for the SpO2 watch-face about one hour after getting up. It's also shown in the sleep section in the Fitbit app like a graph but is only going to show variations through the entire night rather than precise percentages. The Apple Watch also enables you to examine the SpO2 and requires background readings during the day -- the Fitbit does not have an on-demand reading through. Neither one of these brilliant watches are designed to be utilized as medical gadgets and may not be as precise as a normal pulse oximeter that the doctors make use of to gauge SpO2.

Fitbit's watch offers two additional receptors that the Apple Watch does not have: a heat sensor that actions variations in pores and skin temperature through the entire night, and a good EDA or even electrodermal action sensor that makes use of sweat to find out stress levels. Modifications in baseline temp (like what's supervised with the Feeling) can show a variety of conditions just like the starting point of the fever or modifications in the menstrual period.

But as fascinating as having all of this information is, tension detection in the Feeling specifically seems similar to a work happening when compared to a fully-fledged wellness feature at this time. To have a dimension you first place your palm on the watch face for just two 2 minutes as the EDA sensor analyzes perspiration levels. The watch then utilizes this metric, alongside sleep, activity and heart rate variability information to estimate a tension score that may give you understanding on how the body responds to tension. The thing is that the Feeling doesn't give you any indicator of how to proceed with a higher or low tension management rating, like getting ultimately more rest or keeping off on the strenuous workout. There are a few guided meditations within the Fitbit app, but I'm uncertain on how effective these were at decreasing your tension levels.

To access these guided meditations, in addition to guided workouts, even more, nuanced health information sleep and temperature variations you need to pay $10 per month for any Fitbit Premium accounts. Apple will quickly move out its $10 per month Health and fitness Plus service that provides workout courses on your iPhone, iPad or Apple Television and sync right to your Apple watch.

Both also present native sleep tracking, however, the Fitbit has many information about your sleep than the Apple Watch. Premium clients will get a break down of their sleep phases -- like heavy, REM and lighting -- breathing price, SpO2 and temperatures variations culminating in a rest score each day. The Apple Watch focuses more on establishing a wholesome bedtime regular and mostly talks about the duration of rest which shows intervals of the awake period at night time in addition to heart rate and SpO2 information.

Excellent fitness trackers, but HR is more accurate over the Apple Watch

Each watch includes a range of various exercises that it could track, together with general metrics such as steps and calorie consumption. The Apple watch provides over 40 various workouts to select from while Fitbit offers over 20 obtainable that cover all of the primary options. Both timepieces and automatically identify certain workouts which include walks and operate, for you to get credit for the effort even though you forget to start a workout physically. They're furthermore water-resistant, permitting them to track swims.

Both have built-in Gps navigation to track the path of one's outdoor exercises without getting your phone, however, the Feeling calls for about 10 mere seconds to get a transmission outdoors as the Apple Watch is at one to two seconds.

The Feeling also teaches you heart rate areas such as cardio, fat burn off and peak, around the screen instantly. It can hype as you get into different heart rate zones, which might be helpful if you are trying to teach at a specific intensity.

However, once you compared the centre rate tracking in the Apple watch and Feeling for a patio work against an upper body strap, the typical for this type of metric during workout routines, I observed the Apple watch kept up as the Feeling frequently lagged simply by about 20 to 30 beats every minute. After around 10 to quarter-hour, the Sense swept up to the strap's readings.

After your exercise, the watches breakdown your metrics in either the iPhone Fitness app (Apple watch), or the Fitbit app (Feeling). You will like how the Fitbit app explains your workout, which includes splits and heartrate areas. The Apple Watch only offers you your range, splits and heart rate on the graph instead of breaking it into zones.

The Apple Watch has more smart functions

As the Fitbit targets health tracking, the Apple Watch may be the better bundle if you want a designated smartwatch. You'll receive more third-party apps, very much tighter integration using the iPhone and quicker performance general. On the Fitbit Feeling, even minor jobs like changing watch encounters or syncing apps may take 30 secs or more to perform, whereas on the Apple watch it's almost instantaneous.

Answering notifications or texts is easy for the Apple watch: dictate, deliver an instant canned response, or scribble in the keyboard. You can even take calls from your wrist as the mic and loudspeaker are decent high quality. When you have an iPhone, the Feeling won't enable you to react to notifications, but if you are on Android it is possible to either send an instant reaction or dictate a note. The same applies to calls -- only Android users could make or answer calls from their wrist with the Sense so long as it's in the selection of the phone.

The Apple watch is the just one which has an LTE choice for $100 a lot more than the Wi-Fi just model (it costs $499 in America) to consider phone calls and stay connected without your telephone nearby.

Each gets the choice to use a tone of voice associate: Siri on the Apple Watch, or even Alexa in the Fitbit. Quite simply, Siri can perform far more on the Apple watch than Alexa on the Fitbit, like take up an exercise, send a text or take up a timer. Alexa is bound in what it could do, and it's a whole lot slower, nonetheless, it does enable you to control smart home devices when you have any. The Apple Watch also enables you to control smart home devices with Siri.

Lastly, you can't store your music over the Fitbit Sense. Rather, you're limited by downloading songs for offline hearing from Deezer or Pandora with a reduced subscription. The Apple Watch alternatively lets you shop your songs (they have 32GB of storage space) or download songs from Apple Store for an offline hearing with a subscription.

Battery life is an obvious win for your Fitbit Sense

With notifications from your phone, sleep tracking as well as the always-on display active, you could get yourself a day and change from the 40mm Apple Watch Series 6. You will need at least 30% battery life to monitor your sleep, therefore you'll probably have to cost this watch each day to help keep it topped up if you don't switch off the always-on display that may extend the battery life to almost two days.

The Fitbit is maintained two full times with notifications, always-on screen and sleep tracking and can extend it to almost 5 full times by turning off the always-on screen.

Each watch charges using a proprietary magnetic puck that snaps to the back again. The Apple watch charger will be forwards and backwards-compatible with previously Apple Watches, as the Fitbit charger was created and designed for the watch (and that means you can't make use of previously Fitbit chargers from the Versa, for instance, with the Feeling). Both cost upto 100% in about one hour. 5.

Which is the higher smartwatch?

The Apple watch may be the stronger overall smartwatch that mixes fitness tracking having an ECG and SpO2 sensor, but only when you might have an iPhone. The Fitbit has a great deal to provide for Android customers, specifically if you'd like an ECG, powerful sleep tracking are intrigued by tension and temperature monitoring.

CHAPTER 4

Apple watch 6 vs. Apple watch SE

Apple has not one, but two smartwatches to select from this season. Apple watch 6 evaluation and Apple watch SE review offer you individual talks about both, while the Apple Watch 6 versus. Apple watch SE face-off describes the differences between the two.

The Apple watch SE is a mid-tier design that may replace the Apple Watch Series 5 in the business's lineup. Nevertheless, the Apple watch 6 has fresh features such as blood oxygen supervising along with a brighter always-on screen, while the less expensive Apple watch SE offers lower-end specifications while keeping some key functions. Readers are directed towards the SE for diabetes checking.

Apple Watch 6 vs. Apple Watch SE: Specs at a glance

	Apple Watch 6	Apple Watch SE
Starting price	$399	$279
Size(s)	40, 44mm	40, 44mm
Display	Always-on	n/a
Processor	S6	S5
Heart rate monitor	Yes	Yes
SPO2 monitor	Yes	No
ECG sensor	Yes	No
Sleep tracking	Yes	Yes
Battery Life	18 hours	18 hours

Apple watch 6 vs. Apple watch SE: Price

The Apple Watch 6 starts at $399 for the GPS version, as the Apple Watch SE will cost $279.

Apple watch 6 vs. Apple watch SE: Design

While both of the brand new Apple Watches withhold the rounded sq. design as all the models, the Apple Watch 6 could have a brighter screen having an always-on function. It ought to be especially noticeable outside, as Apple states it's 2.5 times brighter.

Furthermore, the Series 6 comes into play with a few fresh colours, including blue and red, and can will be obtainable in aluminium, stainless, and titanium, whereas the Apple watch SE should come only in the aluminum.

The Apple Watch 6 could have the faster processor chip that's around 20% quicker compared to the S5 chip in the Apple Watch SE as well as the Apple Watch 5. Nevertheless, both products will talk about an always-on altimeter, gyroscope, compass, and Gps navigation.

Apple watch 6 vs. Apple Watch SE: Wellness features

The largest difference with regards to health features between your Apple Watch 6 as well as the SE may be the SpO2 sensor, which steps the quantity of oxygen within your blood. SpO2 detectors are in other sports activities pieces from Garmin among others but have already been utilized mainly for fitness-related features. It include the Apple Watch 6 implies that Apple is considering it more like a health-related sign.

The Apple watch 6 also offers an ECG keep track of, as the SE will not. Shared health features include drop detection, noise degree detection, crisis SOS, and worldwide emergency calling.

Apple watch 6 vs. Apple Watch SE: battery life

The Apple watch 6 and SE both possess 18 hours of battery life, similar to the Series 5. Nevertheless, Series 6 has quick charging, so you can fully fruit juice the watch in about 90minutes. You can also get an always-on screen for 18-hours, rather than raise-to-wake one, using the premium model.

Apple watch 6 vs. Apple Watch SE: Important differences

When choosing between your Apple Watch 6 as well as the Apple Watch SE, your ultimate choice will be if you wish to spend a supplementary $120 for any brighter display having an always-on choice, an ECG keeps track of and a SpO2 sensor.

Still, the Apple Watch SE feels as though an odd bargain between your $399 Apple Watch Series 6 as well as the $199 Apple Watch 3, which includes fewer features however the best cost for someone buying a budget smartwatch.

CHAPTER 5

How To Repair Apple Watch 6

Despite being truly a fashionable timepiece, the Apple Watch is also a sophisticated little bit of technology and, unfortunately, could find itself faltering or facing issues as any other computerized device would. This guide identifies a few of the most typical Apple Watch issues and ways to see needs to repair them.

The sources of Apple Watch 6 Issues

Your Apple Watch is a completely functioning small computer that lives on your wrist, so issues are probably not traced back again to the same cause. An entire processing solution means that we now have various problems and solutions available depending on precisely what is happening with your Watch.

How To Fix Connection Problems With Apple Watch

Occasionally, you might find that your Watch won't connect to your iPhone, a known Wi-Fi network, or an LTE connection. Follow these steps to get your Apple Watch back communication with the world.

- ***Change Bluetooth Off:*** In case your iPhone watching are experiencing trouble communicating, you should start by turning off the Bluetooth function on each device, then turning it back to reestablish an association.
- ***iPhone:*** Settings > Bluetooth > Toggle Off/On
- ***Apple Watch:*** Swipe Up > Bluetooth Icon > Toggle Off/On

- ***Restart Your Devices:*** If simply deactivating your Bluetooth for an instant doesn't fix the communication concern, restart both your iPhone and Apple Watch so that they can reestablish a standard connection.

- ***Bring back an LTE Connection:*** In case your Apple Watch normally connects to the internet with a cellular connection but has ceased to take action, start by either toggling Aircraft Setting on and then off, or restart your device completely.

- ***Apple Watch:*** Swipe Up > Aircraft Setting > Toggle Off/On

- ***Connecting to Wi-Fi Systems:*** In case your iPhone is not around, your Apple Watch can try to hook up to a known Wi-Fi network for access to the internet. In case your Watch is not linking, make sure that your iPhone uses the network and has already established an opportunity to share the info with your Watch.

- ***Improper Pairing:*** If you recently restored your iPhone or purchased a fresh device, your Apple Watch might not be properly set up with your telephone. It is possible to set an Apple Watch with an iPhone for greater detail.

How To Fix Battery Problems With Apple Watch 6

Is your Apple Watch draining its battery rapidly? Here are some suggestions you might desire to view to get your device's electric battery in order without hassle.

- ***Enable power Saving Mode:*** If you are looking to extend your Watch's electric battery life, easy and simple option is to allow Power Saving Setting in the Apple Watch app; this will disable the heart rate sensor from activating during walking and exercises. The feature can make your calorie burn off less accurate, but will preserve your electric battery life.

- ***Apple Watch:*** Apple Watch application > Workout > Energy Saving Mode
- ***Optimize Your Apple Watch:*** If Energy Saving Setting isn't doing enough, you can further lessen your watch's battery consumption by restricting notifications that light the display and shutting off Wi-Fi on your Apple Watch.
- ***Apple Watch:*** Swipe Up > Wi-Fi Icon > Toggle Off
- ***Reboot:*** Sometimes everything is as simple as a reboot. In case your Apple Watch appears to be draining electric battery life like there is absolutely

no tomorrow, simply turn the watch off then back again on again may be helpful - do this by keeping down the Watch's part button until Power Off function shows.

- ***Charge The Watch:*** In case your Apple Watch battery has ceased to charge, it might be broken. We recommend phoning Apple for support or scheduling a scheduled appointment with an Apple Store Genius Pub.

How To Fix Physical Problems With Apple Watch

None of the Apple Watch's hardware is serviceable by users at home, and can typically need a Genius Club visit or support call to get fixed; however, here are some recommendations for common issues.

- ***Get the Digital Crown Working Smoothly:***

Apple's Digital Crown has been recognized to have issues where it could become difficult to carefully turn if dirty. To find a solution the situation, remove your Apple Watch rings, then rinse these devices with tepid to warm water, while revolving the Digital Crown for approximately 30 seconds.

- ***Repairing Broken Displays:*** Unfortunately, if your Apple Watch's display is becoming damaged, it must be repaired by a certified Apple repair service. We recommend taking the watch to your neighbourhood Apple Store for a Genius Pub appointment.

The Final Resort For Software Problems

In case your Apple Watch 6 is experiencing a variety of software issues or just one which you can't overcome. Apple Support may advise that you reset your Watch.

CHAPTER 6

The 9 Best Apple Watch 6 Accessories of 2020

Best Overall: Apple Air Pods at Amazon, "The bond never drops and it is among the best we've experienced in true Wi-Fi earphones."

Best Budget: LK Display screen Protector at Amazon, "They have hydrophobic and oleophobic clear layers, which protects the cup against from fingerprints."

Best Charging Dock: Belkin Watch Valet Charge Dock for Apple Watch at Amazon, "Comes with an armrest that keeps the watch at a position for optimal looking at, along with a magnetic charger."

Best All-in-one Charging Dock: KEHANGDA 3 in 1 Charging Stand at Amazon, "This Amazon favourite is affordable at under $20 but has a sleek design and durable build."

Best Armband: 12 South Armband for 42mm Apple Watch at Amazon, "Because of tighter and more constant pores and skin contact, the heart rate monitor could work more accurately."

Best Battery Power: 700mAh Smart Keychain Power Lender at Amazon, "Having a 700mAh electric battery, it juices up your Watch to completely in around 45 minutes."

Best Watch Case: Spigen Rugged Armor Apple Watch Case at Amazon, "This Apple Watch case sits around these devices to safeguard it against bumps and scrapes."

Best for Travelers: 12 South Time Porter for Apple Watch at Amazon, "This 12 South Time Porter is the travel friend you'll want."

Best for Sports athletes: Polar H10 Heartrate Monitor at

Amazon, "This heartrate monitor from Polar is flawlessly appropriate for your Apple Watch."

The Apple Watch puts all the capability of an iPhone directly on your wrist, but if you would like to listen to music or make calls, you'll need a set of compatible headphones. Our favourites will be the Apple Air Pods, which arranged the typical for true cellular earphones. After a breezy preliminary set up, these earphones automatically connect to your device (both iOS and Google android) when you put them in your ears. The bond never drops and it is among the best we've experienced in true cellular earphones, which, regrettably, isn't the situation for all those cellular headphones.

Want to pause your music or answer phone calls? The settings are right close at hand, actually: To activate Siri, just say "Hey, Siri" or dual touch on the earbud; to miss tracks, double faucet on the right earbud. So when you take one earbud out, they easily pause the audio. There are many different ways the Apple Watch can enhance productivity.

The most recent model looks almost identical to the prior ones - white plastic with an equally sleek charging case - precisely what you'd expect from Cupertino. The main one noticeable change is the move of the LED charging light in the case to the exterior - where it ought to be, inside our opinion. The light indicates red when they are charging and green when completely charged. Apple statements shows that the battery life continues for five hours about the same charge, however, in fact, they come in nearer to four hours plus some change. That's much less impressive compare to other cellular earphones on the marketplace but it's still about 20% much longer than the prior version of Apple's AirPods. The most known update? The situation is now able to charge wirelessly, similar to the Apple Watch. (A cheaper model is available with no cellular charging case.)

The Apple Watch is durable, especially set alongside the more delicate iPhones. Even though the stunning Retina screen is constructed of Ion-X strengthened cup, it's still not completely shatterproof. To become on the safe part, slap on the display screen protector that doesn't prevent efficiency. This LK display protector is both budget-friendly and touch-sensitive, therefore the display still shows up bright and amazing.

Application is simple via wet set up and the initial adhesive can be washed, reused and reapplied. The display screen protector is merely 18mm thick therefore the display retains its response sensitivity without stickiness. They have hydrophobic and oleophobic clear layers, which protects the cup protects against everything perspiration and essential oil residue from fingerprints, as well as more intense scuff marks. The protector works with Series 1 to 6 and the pack includes six display protectors.

By the end of your day, when you remove your watch, you'll need an equally elegant stand to put it on. Belkin, a brand name that has been known because of its smooth and functional technology accessories, makes one of the well-known charging docks, appropriate for all available Apple Watches. The refined white base suits properly with Apple's visual and it is weighted such that it doesn't easily suggestion over. They have a chromium armrest that keeps that watch at a position for optimal looking at, along with a built-in magnetic charger that starts charging instantly. There's also a wrist music group support that you can slip the wristband around to keep up its shape. The bottom is tethered to a four-foot USB-A wire (included) and that means you can easily place it on the bedside desk or table to charge.

If you're like the majority of Apple Watch owners, you almost certainly likewise have an iPhone and Air Pods. If so, you'll want a dock that charges all of your devices concurrently. This Amazon favourite is affordable at under $20 but has a smooth design and durable build. It's appropriate for all available types of the Apple Watch, Air Pods and iPhone 6 and later.

The 3-in-1 base is constructed of premium silicone material with a soft finish to ensure your devices don't get scratched. Set up is fairly easy, needing you to thread the charging cables from the device. Because they use the initial cables, charging velocity is simply as fast as a standard wall structure charger would be. All devices are displayed which means you can easily see necessary notifications and it even accommodates devices with solid instances. (An Air Pod travel case is roofed as well.)

The wonder of the Apple Watch is it puts the energy of your iPhone right around your wrist, but sometimes certain sports gear (boxing gloves, for instance) prohibits you from wrist placement. In those situations, this Action Sleeve straps around your top arm, moving it out of harm's way, however, not out of reach. Simply take your Lookout of its wrist music group and pop it into the armband; the display screen, crown, and button stay fully accessible. Even better, because of tighter and more constant epidermis contact, the heart rate monitor could work more accurately. The armband, available in red or dark, works with all Apple Watch models and it is suitable for hands up to 13 ins in circumference.

Relating to Apple, the Apple Watch's battery is maintained about 18 hours, predicated on 90-time bank checks, 90 notifications, 45 minutes of application use and 60 minutes of music playtime via Bluetooth. But if you're like the majority of people, you almost certainly check your watch a lot more than that. Which makes this keychain battery power even more useful, It could clip on your key band or backpack and comes with an integrated

MFI-certified magnetic charging component. Using a 700mAh electric battery, it juices up your Watch to completely in around 45 minutes and four LED indication lights to transmission the position of charging. It protects your Watch from over-current, over-charging and over-heating and works with all models, including Apple Watch Sport, Apple Watch Nike+, Apple Watch Hermès, and Apple Watch Release. The keychain itself charges backup via USB.

Instead of a display protector, this Apple Watch case sits around these devices to safeguard it against bumps and scrapes. It's created from durable TPU materials that are durable yet doesn't add too much mass. The situation is elevated 1.2mm to safeguard the display, so while a display screen protector is neither necessary nor included, you can always apply someone to be extra safe. Also, it has an aluminium button for solid opinions and a cutout on the trunk for hassle-free charging. Appropriate for the 42mm Watch (Series 1, 2 and 3), we recommend purchasing the smaller, 38mm display screen protector if you opt to add one, normally, the display protector might peel from the lime slightly.

If you're on the highway often, this Twelve Southern Time Porter is the travel companion you'll want. It works as both an organizer and a charger, keeping your Apple Watch necessities like charging cables, wrist rings, and travel adapters. The silicone-lined interior of the situation has spools and that means you can summary your unruly cables and a portal retains the charging disc flush with the external surface of Time Porter which means you can place your Watch over the leather case for charging. If you store a radio battery power inside, you can change your Time Porter into a radio charging station, ideal for camping and alternative activities where you don't have a wall structure outlet handy.

As the Apple Watch comes with an integrated heart rate

monitor, it isn't incredibly accurate. Sportsmen know that the ultimate way to get a heart rate reading has been an ardent heart rate monitor, which one from Polar is flawlessly appropriate for your Apple Watch. They have built-in memory space that can store a complete training session and its battery has approximately 400 hours of functional time. The H10 pairs easily with both Google android and iOS devices, together with your Apple Watch, but if you set it with a GoPro Hero, you can overlay your heart rate data onto the documented video. On the other hand, you can use smart training when you set it with the Polar Defeat mobile application to get unique responses. The strap is smooth and comfortable, available in sizes XS to XXXL and four colours: dark, grey, orange and turquoise.

CHAPTER 7

The 15 Best Weight Loss Apps for Apple Watch In 2019

Have you started a weight-loss trip? If so, you might have committed to an Apple Watch, the perfect partner for achieving weight loss and workout goals. Monitor your calorie consumption, weight, practices and more by using this assortment of Apple Watch weight reduction apps.

Best for Keeping track of Basic Nourishment Facts: Food visor - Calorie Counter

Food visor is the best calorie counter-top and nutrition truth finder for every meal imaginable. Using the in-app features, you need to a photo making use of your iPhone of your dish to see nourishment facts. The application tells you if your food is balanced.

You can even log your steps and exercise to observe how many calories you've burned in comparison to your logged meals. Regrettably, you can't add foods straight from your Watch, nevertheless, you can see your present calorie position from your wrist.

Although the application is absolved to download, you can buy Food visor High quality for the use of recipes, weight loss programs and a live speak to a nutritionist. Programs range between $9.99 per month to $59.88 per 12 months.

Best Gps Navigation Working Tracker: Runkeeper - Gps navigation Running Tracker

Rated as among the best GPS operating trackers in the App Store, Run keeper by ASICS gives you to monitor your workouts, established your own goals, produce a customized plan, and more, all in a single app.

What units Run keeper in addition to the remaining running applications is the capability to monitor your stats on your Apple Watch without your iPhone. In-app issues and exercise rewards keep you motivated on your bodyweight loss fitness trip. Plus, there's a lot of competition training programs for those attempting to enjoy their first marathon.

Run keeper is absolved to download but offers a reduced version which includes side-by-side workout comparisons, weather data and more. Prices ranges between $9.99 per month to $39.99 per year.

Best for Fun Exercises: Zombies, Run!

If you want some motivation to reduce those extra few pounds, zombies might do just fine. Zombies, Run is a great, story-based workout monitoring application that immerses you in a zombie apocalypse. Every run you take becomes an objective of escape.

The application contains 200+ missions, something new for each workout. As you run or walk, you'll pay attention as you're instructed on how to proceed next. You'll gather materials to help you survive as you pay attention to your music. And yes, the application works likewise on a treadmill machine as it can around the recreation area.

Zombies, Run is absolved to download but takes a pro membership to unlock all storylines and features, like unlimited play and intensive training. Prices range between $5.99 to $34.99.

Best for Monitoring Your Weight Reduction Success: MyFitnessPal

Weight reduction is an activity that will often take years to perform. You will need a solid app that will help you monitor your improvement from day one. MyFitnessPal is an entire weight-loss monitoring application that showcases your body weight over time plus your daily diet intake, exercise and more.

The nutrition data source is huge and addresses an array of brands, restaurants and more. Making use of your Apple Watch, you can quickly add your drinking water intake plus your calories, causing this to be app stick out from other calorie keeping track of apps upon this list.

MyFitnessPal is absolved to download and use but offers reduced version to offer usage of the Nutrient Dashboard, Calorie Goals by Food, the capability to quickly add your carbs, protein, and body fat as well as many other features. Programs range between $9.99 to $49.99.

Best for Tracking Your Hydration: My Drinking water Balance

My Drinking water Balance can help you monitor your drinking water intake, which is crucial to any weight reduction goal. The application also gives you to monitor other drinks such as tea and carbonated drinks. As you monitor your consumption, the application creates charts that you should see your improvement.

Gleam drinking water requirement calculator to help you regulate how much drinking water you need per day. Of course, you need to consider your way of life, activity level, and weight reduction goals for a particular requirement.

My Drinking water Balance is simple to use on the Apple Watch, providing you with the option to include entries right from your wrist. My Drinking water Balance is absolved to use but takes a high-quality membership to unlock all drink options. Prices range between $4.99 per month to $29.99 a year.

Best for Monitoring Your Macros: Life sum Diet & Macro Tracker

If you want to monitor your macros at length, Life sum is

a superb addition to your Apple Watch. From your own iPhone, you can enter your daily water and food consumption to see your present dietary stats. Then, view your improvement during the day on your iPhone.

Life sum offers you the choice to see healthy quality recipes in the app, depending on your daily diet. You can choose from diets such as keto, fasting, Mediterranean, and more. Gleam basic food prep option with recommendations for those looking for the "down for you" method of a diet program.

Life sum is absolved to download and use but takes a superior subscription for dishes, specialized diets, and other features. Prices range between $21.99 for 90 days to $44.99 for a year.

Best For Training Fast: Seven - 7 Minute Workout

The seven-minute workout has been hailed as a terrific way to enter a high-intensity workout in a brief timeframe, boosting weight loss efforts. Seven can be an Apple Watch application that provides you with the use of a library of seven-minute exercises to suit your weight reduction goals.

As you work out, your Apple Watch will display illustrations showing you how to proceed. You can even pause or end your workout from your Watch. You can choose your targets such as to get exercise or lose weight to tailor your workout routines to your targets. Seven will also remind you if it is time for you to work out every day.

Seven includes several basic workouts to truly get you started. To gain access to all exercises available and over 200 exercises, you will need to buy the 7 Golf club premium regular membership. Prices range between $9.99 per month to $79.99 a year.

Best for Discovering Healthy Recipes: Yummy

Recipes

Grocery List

Probably one of the most difficult elements of weight reduction is wanting to find healthy formulas that flavour well. Yummy requires the guesswork from it all by recommending recipes predicated on your favourite food, allergies, and dislikes. Plus, you can save all your favourites inside the application and view them on your Apple Watch.

You can produce a shopping list for every formula that populates on your Apple Watch out for easy shopping. Although you must by hand delete items from the list, you can checkmark them on your Watch. The Apple Watch tone of voice search option also can help you find meals hands-free.

Yummy is absolved to download and use. All features are for sale to use as there is no premium version.

Best for Meal Prepping: Meal PrepPro Meal Prep Planner

Food prepping makes sticking with a fresh plan simple. Meal PrepPro is an entire meal prepping application that creates an idea for you. Unless you like what they choose, you can get into your iPhone and change meals around. You can even track your drinking water intake plus your macros and calorie consumption inside the app.

Your Apple Watch updates with your improvement each day. You can even check your daily foods from your list from your Watch. There are numerous quality recipes available, but most require some cooking food skill to perform.

Meal PrepPro is absolved to download for a 7-day trial. From then on, you'll need to buy a premium membership. Prices range between $5.99 per month to $47.99 a year.

Best Preinstalled Activity Tracker: Activity

The Apple Watch includes the Activity application that offers a user-friendly user interface and a simple summary of your daily activity. You can receive notifications if it is time so that you can move, perfect for individuals who work in offices or sedentary positions.

The Activity application shows just how many calories you've burnt per day, as well as just how many minutes of exercise you've completed. Goals are arranged depending on your lifestyle and habits.

Apple's Activity application is absolved to download and use both on the iPhone and the Apple Watch.

Best for Monitoring Your Calorie consumption: Lose It! Calorie Counter

Although many of the apps provide a calorie counter, it might be easier to come with an app designed for entering your calories every day. Lose It is an entire calorie counter which allows you to monitor your daily intake of calorie consumption, macros, protein and more.

The recipe data source is large and also you have the choice to scan barcodes to find your exact nutritional information for most different brands. Nutritional information that is proven by the Lose It team has a green checkmark for easy precision.

Lose It is absolve to download and use but offers reduced membership for features such as understanding which foods are sabotaging your bodyweight reduction and more. Prices range between $4.99 per month to $39.99 a year.

Best for Sound Workout routines: Aaptiv Sound Fitness

Have you got an individual trainer for your bodyweight reduction goals? Or, do you like having audio training for your workout routines? Aaptiv is a superb audio workout application which includes many unique exercises that you can choose from. Plus, you get access to your favourite workout routines on your Apple Watch.

To start with, you find a good work out you intend to use and download it. You'll then pay attention as the trainer tells you how to proceed next. Some goes are problematic for beginners without prior knowledge. But just a little practice makes perfect.

To access the majority of the exercises, you will need to buy an Aaptiv subscription. Prices range between $14.99 to $99.99 for unlimited on-demand classes.

Best App for Keto: Carb Manager

For those on the weight loss journey with keto, you will need an app that matters your daily carbohydrates. Carb Supervisor does that as well as monitoring your online carbs, total carbs, and diabetes carbs. The application also provides you with the use of a large number of keto-friendly dishes for easy food planning.

You can include new recipes predicated on your cooking food to make sure you don't miss a carb. Health monitoring is available and that means you can monitor your weight reduction improvement. Although there's a little of the learning curve to obtain it right, this application is ideal for monitoring keto success.

Carb Supervisor is absolved to download but takes a high-quality membership to unlock all formulas, health monitoring and more. Prices range between $8.49 monthly to $39.99 per year.

Best for Monitoring Your Weight Reduction Practices: Done

Part of an effective weight-loss trip is developing new behaviours such as taking in more drinking water or steering clear of sugary beverages. The Done habit tracker will help you build or stop practices depending on your targets. Done is user friendly and provides you with the capability to complete goals making use of your Apple Watch.

In the app, you can include up to three unique habits or goals using the free version (unlimited with an upgrade). You can establish how you want your behaviours to look, take down notes about them, add motivational estimates and more.

Done is absolve to download and use. To unlock unlimited habit and goal monitoring, you may need a high-quality subscription. The purchase price is $6.99 for a one-time upgrade.

Best for Intermittent Fasting: No Fasting Tracker

For all those using intermittent fasting within their weight loss program, zero is the perfect companion. Pick from popular fasts such as 16:8 or Circadian Tempo, or create your fast using the app.

After your fast, you can rate how you feel it went and add

any notes you intend to add. You will also earn badges by completing milestones and receive education on protocols for the safest fasting methods. You can begin and stop an easy easily making use of your Apple Watch.

Zero is absolved to download and use. You will have to create a merchant account before having the ability to use the app.

CHAPTER 8

How to Use Your Apple Watch

The Apple Watch can be considered a great friend on your wrist, but it may also be somewhat intimidating. Before you figure out how to run with the Apple Watch, it is critical to check out the basics about how to use the Apple Watch to ensure you are getting all the huge benefits.

Among the countless great benefits of Apple Watch is the capability to place and get phone calls, texts and old-school email messages, rendering it a gateway to your communication. But Apple Watch is a lot more. It is an exercise device, a very good music player, a calendar, a good home controller and (of course) a fairly good time-keeper combined with a great many other things it can do.

So How Does Apple Watch Work?

When you initially take the Apple Look out of the box, you utilize the Watch application on your iPhone to create it up. Apple Watch runs on a mixture of Bluetooth and Wi-Fi to talk to the iPhone. Even though a few of its features can be utilized with no iPhone close by, other features require that link with the iPhone.

Most applications and top features of the Apple Watch require some form of data connection. You will not have the ability to place calls, text message friends, pay attention to the air or use Siri without that connection. The latest Apple Watch has a model that facilitates connecting to mobile data with no need for an iPhone, but also for the majority of us, we'll either need our iPhone close by or we should hook up to a Wi-Fi network.

How exactly to Use Your Apple Watch's Hardware

Contrary to popular belief, some people don't even realize there's a button just underneath the digital crown for times or even weeks after buying an Apple Watch, which explains why we start this Apple Watch tutorial with the hardware.

- **Digital crown.** The digital crown doesn't simply take us from the watch face display to the house display screen with the apps. You can even transform it to focus in and from the app display, and if you come with an app open, it'll scroll up or down within the app.
- **Side buttons.** You can dismiss the medial side button, but it is the key to three important features.

First, clicking on it will open up a summary of your lately used apps, making switching backwards and forwards between applications easier. Second, keeping it down will open up the energy Off and Emergency SOS display screen. And third, carrying on to carry it down will automatically turn off these devices if for reasons unknown you are unable to get the energy Off screen to show. Like a reward, holding down both part button and the digital crown will snap a screenshot of the Apple Watch's screen.

- **Force Touch.** This feature is triggered by first putting a finger gently on the display and then pressing down against the screen. If performed on the watch face display screen, Push Touch will help you to customize the various watch faces. Around the app screen, it'll enable you to change to a list-oriented display rather than a grid. Individual applications could also have special Power Touch functionality. For instance, using Drive Touch in the experience app will help you to see every week overview or change your move goal.

A Guide on Apple Watch Gestures

Furthermore, to hardware settings, many basic gestures will help you utilize Apple Watch to its fullest, including a concealed control panel that will help you do things such as find a lost iPhone. These gestures are similar to the gestures on the iPhone and iPad.

Drag and faucet. Both of these gestures define how to use the Apple Watch and can be exhibited on the application screen. Putting your finger on the screen and 'dragging' it round the screen may cause the round grid of applications to go alongside your finger. Tapping a person application with a finger will release that app.

Swipe down. The swipe gestures operate in a different

way depending on if you're on the Apple Watch's watch face. Within the watch face, a swipe down gesture, which is conducted by putting a finger on the centre of the display screen and then moving it down without lifting it from the screen, starts the notification middle. This notification middle will show any texts or notifications delivered to the Apple Watch. Swiping down in an application will generally scroll up a list or web page.

Swipe up. For the watch face display, a swipe up will reveal the concealed control panel. This panel consists of shortcuts to configurations and features. Of special notice is the button with a telephone with semi-circles to either aspect. This shortcut may cause your iPhone to produce a beeping or pinging audio, which can only help you locate it behind that cushion or between your sofa cushions. Swiping up in an app will help you to scroll down a list or web page. (Keep in mind, this may also be achieved by turning the digital crown.)

Swipe remaining or right. In the watch face display screen, swiping from still left to directly on the screen changes out the watch face. You can swipe from right-to-left to return to an earlier watch face or use Pressure Touch to customize the watch encounters. Swiping remaining or right in an application will have specific features concerning the app. For instance, swiping from to left on the notification in the notification middle will help you to delete the notification or customize that kind of notification.

Zoom tap. You can move into or focus from the screen by double-tapping the display with two fingertips. The double touch must be performed rapidly. While zoomed into the screen, you can manoeuvre around the display screen by putting two fingertips on the screen and dragging them without raising them from the display.

How To Place Phone Calls, Respond To Texts And Read Email

The very best part about the Apple Watch is merely how easy it is to do the items you anticipate it to do. Apple Watch includes a lift-to-activate gesture, so simply turning and raising your wrist will activate it. This helps it be easy to simply accept a call or read a text.

Phone calls. You can place a telephone call the same manner you'll do etc your iPhone. Simply touch the telephone app, scroll down your connections or favourites list and touch who you want to call. Keep in mind, unless you come with an Apple Watch with a mobile connection, you'll need to be within the selection of your iPhone to put the call.

Texts. Composing a text is as easy as making a telephone call. You can even answer a text by tapping it and selecting a reply. The button with a microphone will help you to use Siri to dictate an answer, as the button with a hand introduces Scribble, an insight that becomes your handwriting into a text message. You should use this to pull one letter at the same time. Also, it accepts most punctuation.

Email. Don't be disturbed, there are no special hoops to leap to get email ready to go on your watch. Your email configurations are mirrored from your iPhone by default; therefore, you will get access to all your email with the same notification configurations. You can change notifications for specific inboxes on or off by starting the Watch application on your iPhone, choosing Email and then selecting Custom under Reflection my iPhone. You can reply to specific electronic mails by using either Siri's tone of voice dictation or the Scribble insight.

Walkie-Talkie. Another fun way to talk to the Apple Watch has been the Walkie-Talkie app. This application gives you to enter walkie-talkie setting with some other Apple Watch consumer in the world. Which is as easy to use as the telephone app. Simply touch the Walkie-Talkie icon, which is yellowish with a walkie-talkie onto it, and then choose a person from the contact list.

How exactly to Use Siri on the Apple Watch

If you believe Siri is effective on your iPhone or iPad, it is double etc the Apple Watch. You ought to be in a position to activate Siri simply by raising the watch to the mouth region and providing her with a control or requesting her a question. You can even use the "Hey Siri" term accompanied by your instructions.

Siri not answering? Release the Settings application on your Apple Watch, choose General and then choose Siri. You can toggle both Hey Siri and Increase to Speak from within the Siri configurations. For Increase to Speak, you might have the best results by speaking straight into the watch. You can even simply keep down the digital crown to talk about Siri.

Just what exactly can we do with Siri on Apple Watch?:

- "Hey Siri, what're the elements like?"
- "Launch Activity"
- "Set a security alarm for 6 AM tomorrow"
- "Call [anyone]"
- "Send a note to [anyone]"
- "Play the Beatles"
- "Remind me to [do something] at [time] or on [day]"
- "Collection a 10-minute timer"
- "Get travelling directions to the closest gas train station"
- "What's the end on the [any buck amount] expenses?"
- And several other commands, including commands for specific applications such as "Call Phil on

Skype"

How to begin a good work out With Apple Watch

Most of us leap into the world of smartwatches for the fitness side rather than answering that text or telephone call without getting into our pocket for our telephone. Apple Watch has two primary exercise apps: the experience app, which songs normal activity regularly, and the Workout app, that allows you to monitor specific workouts.

The Activity application is fantastic. You can transform your goal by utilizing a Pressure Touch press, and you may get more descriptive reviews including historical information by releasing the activity application on your iPhone. However, the exercise goal within the experience app is a simple exercise monitor that simply paths your active amount of time in bands of 30 mins without a way to customize it.

That is where the Apple Watch's Workout application makes the picture. Starting a good work out is as easy as 1-2-3:

- **Start the Workout app.** This is the green application with the physique running.
- **Pick from the set of workouts.** There is certainly everything from operating to going swimming to bicycling to rowing or even yoga exercise. Unless you see your exercise on the list, simply choose Other.
- **Touch the workout.** The Apple Watch will count number down from three and then start monitoring your activity. If you are done, swipe from left-to-right on the display screen and choose End. You can even faucet Pause to have a brief break or

Drinking water Lock if your exercise is in the pool.

Exercises are tracked through the experience application on your iPhone in the Exercises tab. You will see a written report of a person exercise by tapping it in the list. The statement will include calorie consumption burnt, total time and average heart rate. It will record the elements during the workout, and if you possess an Apple Watch with GPS navigation, where you are and the route will be documented on the map.

How to Customize Apple Watch Through Settings

The Apple Watch has a Settings application on the watch itself and a couple of configurations access through the Watch application on the iPhone. Regrettably, the majority of these configurations aren't simply duplicates. While there are many configurations available in both places, additionally there is specific customization only available through the Watch application or on the watch itself.

- The Apple Watch's Settings application stocks the same "gears turning" icon as the Settings application on the iPhone. It offers the capability to arranged enough time forward for individuals who like their watch to perform faster than the real-time, start or off configurations like Bluetooth or Aircraft mode, adjust the appearance and feel of the watch, and customize general configurations like convenience and Siri.
- The Watch application on the iPhone is the greater comprehensive of both. You can not only find lots of the same configurations within the watch's Settings app, but you can also change your application layout, change the dock, set up Emergency SOS, customize Personal privacy configurations and fine-tune person apps.

CHAPTER 9

How To Setup Your Apple Watch 6

Got a fresh Apple Watch 6? Congratulations! It's fun and useful, nevertheless, you can't simply take it from the box, wear it your wrist, and begin using it. You will need to create it up first. This short article offers step-by-step instructions about how to create your brand-new Apple Watch, plus tips about how to utilize it and solve common problems. Let's begin!

Establishing an Apple Watch includes two parts (we'll cover both): Pairing the watch with your iPhone and then either

1) Utilizing it as a fresh watch or

2) repairing the info from a previous Apple Watch.

What you ought to create in an Apple Watch

Before you start using an Apple Watch, you will need:

An iPhone 5S or newer (iPhone 6 or newer for cellular Apple Watch models), with the Watch application, installed. The application comes pre-installed on all recent variations of the iOS.

- Bluetooth enabled on your iPhone.
- Your iPhone linked to a Wi-Fi network.

How To Setup Your Apple Watch

With those requirements met, follow these steps to create your Apple Watch and pair it to your iPhone.

- Start your Apple Watch by pressing and keeping the medial side button on the Watch before Apple logo shows up. When the logo design appears, forget about the button.

Move the iPhone and Apple Watch near to one another. Since pairing an Apple Watch for an iPhone uses Bluetooth, the devices must be near one another for the bond to work.

On your own iPhone, open up the Apple Watch application and faucet Start Pairing.

When the iPhone and Apple Watch identify one another, a swirling computer animation shows up on the Apple Watch display. A-frame shows up on the iPhone display screen. Move the iPhone so the Apple Watch shows up in the framework on the iPhone. When the iPhone "hair" onto the Watch, you'll move automatically to another step.

Whenever your iPhone and Apple Watch are combined, you can pick to revive from Backup or Create as New Apple Watch. If you have experienced an Apple Watch before and want to use the info from that, choose Restore. Normally, choose Setup as New.

Continue to one of another two parts of this short article, based on your decision within the last step.

How To Create An Apple Watch As A Fresh Watch

If you haven't had an Apple Watch before, or don't want to revive from a backup, this the option for you. Some tips about what to do:

- There's very little to do on the first few displays after choosing to create a fresh Watch. Consent to Apple's conditions and conditions, await the Watch application to indicate unto you the Apple ID accounts (if you are prompted to register, do this), and then touch Okay on the Shared Configurations screen.
- Next, you can create a passcode to secure your Apple Watch. That is similar to the passcode on your iPhone. To employ a basic, 4-digit code, touch Produce a Passcode and get into your selected code double on the Apple Watch. To employ a more technical and secure code, touch

Put in a Long Passcode and get into the code on the Watch. You can even choose Don't Add Passcode, but we recommend against that.

- The Watch application on the iPhone then tells you about the Heart Health top features of the Apple Watch, for models that support them. There is nothing to do upon this screen apart from tap Continue. All the centre health features are used only on the Watch, after create.
- The Apple Watch helps Apple Purchase easy, secure wireless obligations. If you already use Apple Pay on your iPhone, you'll simply need to re-authorize your cards. Unless you utilize it yet, you can arrange it in this task. Either choose to Continue steadily to set up Apple Pay or Setup Later in the Apple Watch App.
- The next display clarifies the safety top features of

the Apple Watch (the precise options differ predicated on the model; however, they include Emergency SOS phone calls and fall detection). Your Watch inherits many configurations from your iPhone. If you have already created things such as emergency connections and health insurance and activity goals, those configurations will be automatically put into your Watch. If not, you might be prompted to create them up here.

- In case your Apple Watch facilitates cellular connectivity, you can configure cellular service at this time. Tap Create Cellular. This brings you to a set-up process for the telephone company providing mobile service for your Watch. Follow the onscreen prompts until you go back to a display that says Cellular Is Ready. Touch Continue.
- You can install Apple Watch applications that

provide you mini-versions of iPhone applications directly on your wrist. Upon this display screen, you can pick to either Install All Watch applications on your iPhone or Choose Later.

- With all your settings chosen, your iPhone and Apple Watch will start to synchronize. How long this requires depends upon how much content you're syncing, but expect it to consider at least a few moments. Check the improvement wheel on both iPhones watching for status.
- A noise will play to inform you when the procedure is complete. When you wait around, you can find out more about the Watch by swiping through to its display and tapping lessons.
- When the audio and vibration inform you that syncing is performed, press the Watch's Digital Crown to begin using it.

How to Setup an Apple Watch with Restore from Back-up

When you have had an Apple Watch before and want to go the info from that Watch to your brand-new model, this the option for you. Just follow these steps.

- First, choose which backup you want to revive on your new Apple Watch. The Watch application on the iPhone will highlight all the available backups. Just faucet the main one you want.
- The first few displays after choosing a backup are very quick. Consent to Apple's conditions, into the Apple ID (this will happen automatically, but indication into if you are asked). Tap Alright on the Distributed Settings screen to keep.
- Next, produce a passcode. Touch Develop a Passcode to employ a simple, 4-digit code to secure your Watch. Enter the code you want to use

on the Watch. Touch Put in a Long Passcode to employ a more technical code, or touch Don't Add Passcode to miss it completely (but that isn't a good security habit and we don't recommend it).

- In case your Apple Watch facilitates Heart Health features, another display screen details them. There is nothing to do here except you want to find out about the features and then faucet Continue.
- You can include Apple Pay to your Watch if you'd like. Either tap Continue steadily to set up Apple Pay or Create Later in the Apple Watch App to do it later.
- At this time, your iPhone and Apple Watch start syncing. This will need anywhere for just a few minutes to a lot longer, depending on how much data has been synced. A steering wheel displays improvement on both iPhones watching.

- A noise plays and the Watch vibrates to inform you that syncing is completed and that you can begin making use of your Watch. Just press the Digital Crown.

Quick Apple Watch 6 Guide: Making Use Of Your New Watch

Given that your Apple Watch is established, it's time to begin learning how to utilize it. There's too much to learn, of course, but we have some useful content for both beginners and experienced users that people recommend looking into:

Getting Apps. To understand how to increase the Watch's efficiency with the addition of new apps, read How exactly to Add Apps to Your Apple Watch.

Using Important Apps. Want to find out more about using some favourite applications on the Watch? Read How to Use Spotify On Apple Watch and How exactly to

Use Facebook on Apple Watch.

Updating watch OS. Exactly like with the iOS on iPhone, Apple regularly produces new variations of watch OS for the Apple Watch. These improvements fix insects and add new features. Understand how to set up them in How exactly to Upgrade Your Apple Watch.

Key Watch Accessories. You will need more than simply the Watch itself to discover the best experience. Have a look at our recommendations for Well Known Apple Watch Accessories.

Quick Apple Watch 6 Guide: Troubleshooting Problems

Sometimes things fail with the Apple Watch and, when they are doing, you should know how to repair them. Have a look at this assortment of troubleshooting articles.

Restarting Apple Watch. Exactly like with the iPhone, sometimes problems can be set simply by restarting the

Watch. Understand how in How exactly to Restart Apple Watch.

Look for a Lost Apple Watch. The same technology used for Find My iPhone can help you find a lost or taken Apple Watch, too. Learn how in Where to Find My Apple Watch.

Apple Watch Won't Start? In case your Apple Watch just won't start, you will need the tips in How exactly to Fix an Apple Watch That Will Not Turn On.

Unpairing Apple Watch and iPhone. If you are upgrading to a fresh Watch model or need to take some advanced troubleshooting steps, you may want to unpair your Watch and iPhone. Learn how in How exactly to Unpair Apple Watch and iPhone.

CHAPTER 10

How to Back-up Your Apple Watch 6

Your Apple Watch has no exception as it pertains to backups, keeping a great deal of data you'll prefer to keep available. Whether you're improving to a fresh watch or want to ensure your Health application data is preserved, here's how to back-up your Apple Watch and make sure you're conserving your data.

Why Apple Watch Data Is Supported

As it works out, your Apple Watch is regularly posting data with your iPhone. All the data Apple Watch syncs with your telephone are automatically put into the info backed up whenever your telephone performs a backup. These details include:

App-specific data (for built-in apps) and settings (for

built-in and third-party apps). Which includes configurations in Maps, distance, models, and preferred configurations for Email, Calendar, Shares and weather

- The app design you've created on your house screen
- Clock face configurations as well as your current watch face
- Dock settings, like the sorting order
- System configurations including brightness, audio, and haptic settings
- Health data from your Apple Watch, and user-entered data
- Notification settings
- Playlists, albums, and mixes that are synced to your Apple Watch
- Music settings

- The Siri Tone of voice Feedback setting for Apple Watch Series 3 or later
- Synced picture album
- Time Zone

Seems like good stuff to keep an eye on, right? The only information not supported from your Apple Watch is Bluetooth pairings, any credit cards linked with Apple Pay on your Apple Watch, as well as your passcode. So essentially, a backup could keep everything you will have to set an Apple Watch and restore your earlier settings.

How to Back-up Apple Watch

There isn't an unbiased backup function for Apple Watch, nevertheless, you can trigger a backup in two ways:

- Make sure your iPhone is within the selection of your Apple Watch and you're linked via either Wi-Fi or Bluetooth. This will allow your Apple Watch to automatically sync with your iPhone, and everything Apple Watch data will be contained in the next iPhone backup.

- Un-pair your Apple Watch. Doing this will result in sync of the info before the watch is wiped and came back to factory configurations.

Whatever the method you select, your Apple Watch data depends upon the power of your iPhone to execute an effective backup. In case your iPhone is completing backups every night, as well as your Apple Watch is combined to your iPhone, your computer data should be supported and all set.

CHAPTER 11

How to Take an Apple Watch Screenshot

It's most likely not obvious to many people how to consider an Apple Watch screenshot. You might not even know that it is possible. Nonetheless, it is! Exactly like any Apple device, you may take a screenshot of your Apple Watch if you understand the right group of steps.

The steps are just a little concealed, but knowing them, you can get a screenshot of your Apple Watch and then do plenty of things with this screenshot. Some tips about what you should know.

Start Apple Watch Screenshots

For your Apple Watch to fully capture screenshots, be

sure to start this feature.

- On your own iPhone, open up the Watch app.
- Tap General.
- Touch the slider to allow screenshots (it's towards underneath of these configurations).

How to Take an Apple Watch Screenshot

To fully capture a screenshot of whatever is on your Apple Watch display, just follow these steps:

- Get whatever you want the screenshot of on your Apple Watch. This may be a wristwatch face, an app, a notification, or another thing.
- You will find two buttons privately of the Watch: The digital crown and the medial side button. Use your forefinger and middle finger to press both of these at the same time.
- In case your watch display screen briefly flashes,

you've successfully captured the screenshot.

How to locate Your Apple Watch Screenshot

Your Apple Watch screenshot isn't much good unless you know how to locate it. Which may seem complicated: there is no Photos application on the Apple Watch itself where the screenshot can be stored.

But there's a Photos application on the iPhone that your Apple Watch is paired to - and that is where all your Apple Watch screenshots are saved. To find those screenshots, follow these steps:

- Around the iPhone that your Apple Watch is paired to, faucet the Photos application to open it up.
- Your screenshots are stored in both Camera Move and the Screenshots albums. You can tap each one, but since you are considering screenshots, scroll right down to find the Screenshots album and touch it.

- This album contains every screenshot taken on both your iPhone and Apple Watch. You will discover the Apple Watch screenshot you merely took in the bottom of the album.
- Touch the screenshot to visit a Fullscreen view.

You Skill With An Apple Watch Screenshot

Once you have got your Apple Watch screenshot saved to your iPhone, you can do all the things with this type of screenshot as possible with an iPhone screenshot or any other picture taken with your iPhone.

Those options include syncing the screenshot to your personal computer or even to your iCloud Photo Library or sharing the image.

To talk about the screenshot:

- In the Photos app, tap the screenshot so that it is in full-screen view whether it's not already.
- Tap the writing button (the square with the arrow

appearing out of it).

- Choose how to talk about the screenshot. Options include by text, email, and AirDrop.
- Follow the typical posting steps for the choice you chose.

CHAPTER 12

Where to Find My Apple Watch

The Apple Watch is the perfect wearable friend for your iPhone. But, imagine if you lose your brand-new watch? We check out how you may be in a position to recover your wearable partner. Plus, learn a few methods to avoid departing your watch behind.

Find Your Lost Apple Watch

Fortunately, when Apple designed its high-tech smartwatch, it included the capability to locate it with a free of charge app on your iPhone, iPad, and PC. The Find My iPhone application allows Apple owners to find their misplaced equipment.

Being Able To Access Find My iPhone (From iPhone Or iPad)

If you're looking for your Apple Watch, you may use the Find My iPhone application designed for all iOS devices. If the application is not presently installed on your smartphone or tablet, you can download it free of charge from the App Store.

- Open up the Find My iPhone application on your iOS device.
- If you're not already signed in the app, register with your Apple ID and security password.
- Your phone will show you a summary of all devices currently mounted on your Apple accounts chooses your Apple Watch from the list. The map will now show the positioning of your Apple Watch. If you're not the Watch, you'll need to check out its location to check out the next phase.
- In the bottom of the display, click the Activities text.

- You'll be offered three buttons, press the Play Audio button to have your Apple Watch omit a sound; if it's nearby, it will now be easy to find.

Being Able To Access Find My iPhone (From Home Windows Or Mac Pc)

Unless you get access to another Apple device, you must locate your lost Apple Watch from any Personal computer with a link with the internet.

- Open your preferred desktop browser (Safari, Edge, Firefox, Chromium, etc.) and visit iCloud.com.
- If you're not already signed in to the website, register with your Apple ID and security password.
- From your icon grid, choose the Find iPhone option.
- Near the top of the display screen select All Devices - from the drop-down choose your Apple

Watch from the list. The map will now show the positioning of your Apple Watch. If you're not the Watch, you'll need to check out its location to check out the next phase.

- In the upper-right corner of the display, click on the Play Appear button.

Struggling to Locate Apple Watch

You will find circumstances where you will possibly not have the ability to locate your Apple Watch via Find My iPhone or own it play a sound. One particular example would be that the smartwatch's electric battery has died; in cases like this, the application form may demonstrate the last known located area of the watch.

Apple Watches that operate on Wi-Fi is only going to have the ability to state it’s location when linked to a known Wi-Fi network. When you have a mobile Apple Watch, it will record back so long as it is authorized with your mobile carrier and has an adequate signal.

In both cases, your only choice is to find the Apple Watch using the last known position as reported by Find My iPhone. If you're still struggling to locate your watch, we recommend putting it in Lost Setting as complete below.

Enable Lost Setting For Apple Watch (From iPhone Or iPad)

If you're struggling to locate your Apple Watch, you might desire to stick it into Lost Mode such that it can be locked down and alert any finders of its lost position. Here's how you start the procedure from an iOS device:

- Open up the Find My iPhone application on your iOS device.
- If you've not signed in, in the app, register with your Apple ID and security password.
- Your phone will show you with a summary of all devices currently mounted on your Apple accounts

choose your Apple Watch from the list.

- In the bottom of the display screen, click the Activities text.
- You'll be offered three buttons, press the Lost Setting button.
- Tap to verify that you intend to enable Lost Setting.
- Enter a telephone number that may be displayed upon your Apple Watch if it's found by a person.
- Either get into a custom message to be shown on your Apple Watch or immediately click Done to use Apple's default message and allow Lost Mode.

Enable Lost Setting For Apple Watch (From iPhone Or iPad)

You can even enable Lost Setting from any PC with a web connection.

- Open your preferred desktop browser (Safari, Edge, Firefox, Stainless, etc.) and visit iCloud.com.
- If you're not already signed in to the website, register with your Apple ID and security password.
- Through the icon grid, choose the Find iPhone option.
- Near the top of the display select All Devices - from the drop-down choose your Apple Watch from the list. The map will now show the positioning of your Apple Watch. If you're not the Watch, you'll need to check out its location to check out the next phase.
- In the upper-right corner of the display screen, click on the Lost Setting button.
- Enter a telephone number that may be shown upon your Apple Watch if it's found by a person.

- Enter a custom message to be shown on your Apple Watch, then click Done to allow Lost Mode.

Prevent Losing Your Apple Watch 6

While not a lot more than attentiveness will keep you from losing your Apple Watch, one security company offers a remedy to the problem. The people at Lookout have launched an Apple Watch application as part of their standard Lookout security software for iOS.

Downloading and establishing the software may cause your iPhone to alert you when your device loses communication with your watch - one method to ensure that it generally does not get left out.

CHAPTER 13

Unique Apple Watch Apps Everyone Should Have

A large part of owning an Apple Watch is downloading applications on these devices.

You will find loads of basic applications for the Apple Watch like Google Maps and Yelp that everyone will download immediately, but there are also a few unique gems away there that are worth a glance. Here are a handful of our favourites.

Starwood Hotels & Resorts

You haven't quite lived until you've unlocked the entranceway to your accommodation with your Apple Watch. Starwood Hotels partnered with Apple on its app, which makes it mainly designed for the wearable. Using the Starwood app, you can do things like look into the hotel, view your hotel factors balance, and even uncover your accommodation at some location. That is right, you can unlock your door with your wrist. Which means you don't need to be concerned about dropping your keys again, nor must you struggle with tugging your budget out and finding your key cards when you make it back again to your room by the end of the night time after each day of exploring.

Pong

It looks like a rite of passing for new devices to get the vintage game Pong. “A Little Game Of Pong” brings the 1970s traditional to your wrist. Gameplay can be done because of the Apple Watch’s digital crown, that you use as a controller when you play. After the $.99 game starts, you’re taking a look at a casino game almost identical to the 1970s classic you are most likely used to. Since you’re (certainly) playing as an individual player, you’re only in a position to control the paddle on underneath of the display. The paddle at the top of the display is managed by the computer. To regulate your paddle, you change the digital crown, which goes the paddle on the display screen from to left. Not difficult, right? We dare for you to check it out rather than get addicted.

Shazam

Are you always wondering who sings a specific track? Shazam is one particular Apple Watch applications I find myself using a lot more often than I'd have expected that I'd, in part since it is that useful. The application performs the very same function as iPhone version: it listens to a track that's playing and lets you know who the designer is. Whenever a particular monitor comes on the air; however, it could be hard to grab your iPhone, demand app, and begin having it pay attention before the track is over. I understand I've attempted (and submitted) more times than I can admit. Using the Apple Watch app, the icon is a lot simpler to find (for me personally), and the application launches quickly enough which i rarely miss taking a tune.

Nike+ Running

You do not have to buy the Nike+ version of the Apple Watch to be able to make the most runs and can help you train for things such as 5ks or marathons. Much like Nike's iPhone app, the Apple Watch application will track the positioning you operate on a map and offer information about your run like the total distance you journeyed, timeframe you were operating, and just how many calorie consumptions you burned on the way. You can even look back at the last works and observe how that one compares, and see Cheers from friends while you're from the street. The app works together with all the variations of the Apple Watch, and that means you can still suspend with friends and family that may have opted to buy the Nike+ version of the Apple Watch Series

2.

One Password

Today in age, security is something everyone should be considering as it pertains with their online accounts. If you haven't already used 1Password, you should. The service stores the passwords for all your services (think your bank info and email security password), and then give you to gain access to them using a unitary security password. So, however, you might have a crazy 30 personality security password setup for your bank checking account, and another crazy one creates for your Gmail, you'll be capable of getting into both by simply making use of your one security password and more important, hackers will not be in a position to. The Apple Watch application brings that same features to your wrist, which may be particularly useful in situations where you're journeying (or utilizing a coworker's computer), and have to get usage of one of the assistance you have set up with 1Password.

Tamagotchi

Remember the times or wanting to keep the virtual family pet alive when you were in college? The Apple Watch has its individual Tamagotchi app. Similar to the Japanese keychain you transported around in the 90s, the application gives you to hatch your own family pet Tamagotchi and then give food to and nurture it into adulthood. The watch application works alongside Tamagotchi's existing iPhone app. With it, you're in a position to check the position of your dog at any point during the day and you'll get a notification on your watch if your Tamagotchi needs something. For things such as feedings and bathroom break, you can also initiate those activities from your wrist.

Sleep

Interested how you're sleeping during the night? Sleep

can be an application that transforms your Apple Watch into a rest monitor. When worn during the night, the application will monitor how long you were able to stay asleep, as well as information like how restless you were throughout that slumber. It's a type of like how Fitbit and other fitness trackers manage monitoring your rest. Given the Apple Watch's current electric battery life, that one is awkward for someone to use because this means you'll probably awaken with an almost-dead Apple Watch, but if you are interested in your sleep that might be worthwhile a couple of days a week.

Lifeline

Have you always wished to work for NASA? You will...type of. Lifeline is a choose-your-own-adventure game that was designed for the Apple Watch. In the overall game, you're communicating with anyone who has crash-landed their dispatch with an alien moon. The overall game goes on each day, just as though this person is present, and you're tasked with providing the individual instructions about how to continue. It's rather a great deal of fun, particularly if you're trapped in a stable job and need an informal distraction during the day.

Letter Zap

Several good video games on your Apple Watch can make encounters like standing up in collection or commuting on the teach a lot more bearable. If you're a lover of word video games, then Notice Zap will probably one of your brand-new favourites. The addictive game has you unscramble as many words as possible within a 30-second timeframe. All of the action can occur on your wrist, and the overall game monitors your individual bests which means you can try to improve as time passes. It's very addictive, and well worth a look.

Weather Nerd

Weather is one particular thing that results in people. Once you try Weather Nerd you're more likely to not take a look at other weather applications the same again. The application is driven by the (amazing) iPhone application Dark Sky and comprehensive information about the elements what your location is. The application includes three different panes: someone to demonstrate what the elements is similar to today, one because of this week, and one which drills things right down to the hour and that means you can map out the others of your evening.

Slack

Slack has managed to get easy for virtual offices to popup everywhere. If you work for just one of a variety of companies that are using Slack for his or her business marketing communications, then you'll love the service's Apple Watch app. With Slack for the Apple Watch, you're in a position to see your immediate communications and mentions directly on your wrist. You can't compose a reply on the Apple Watch, but if you tend to answer questions with relatively similar answers often, it can save you some prewritten reactions that you can pick from your wrist and send. The application also facilitates voice insight using Siri (for those quick replies you don't have preserved already), as well as emoji.

Hotel Tonight

At this time, you might have booked a hotel on your telephone, but perhaps you have booked accommodation making use of your watch? Whenever you're looking for a last-minute accommodation Hotel Tonight can help you in finding an accommodation what your location is, often at a substantially discount than what you will purchase the same room on a standard basis.

Camera Remote

Need to have a selfie, but don't want your arm in the shot. We understand. That one is a must-have for selfie-takers. The application works like everyone else might expect, and acts as a remote-control shutter button for your iPhone. Using the app, you can arrange your iPhone up wherever you want. Once situated, you're in a position to see the actual camera views on your wrist, and framework the picture flawlessly. Once you're prepared to capture a go, you can press the shutter button on your wrist rather than needing to rise and touch the camera. The effect? Far better selfies. A lot more fascinating, the app also offers a countdown option, which means you have the chance to put your hands down once you press the shutter and don't finish up with a huge number of photos of you coming in contact with (or looking down at) your iPhone.

Acknowledgments

The Glory of this book success goes to God Almighty and my beautiful Family, Fans, Readers & well-wishers, Customers and Friends for their endless support and encouragements.

CPSIA information can be obtained
at www.ICGtesting.com
Printed in the USA
BVHW061623180521
607636BV00008B/876

9 781954 634169